Dissertation Skills for Business and Management Students

Dissertation Skills

for Business and Management Students

Brian White

CONTINUUM
London and New York

Continuum
The Tower Building
11 York Road
London SE2 7NX

370 Lexington Avenue
New York
NY 10017-6550

First published 2000
Reprinted 2000

British Library Cataloguing-in-Publication Data

A catalogue record for this book is available from the British Library.

ISBN 0-8264-5392-9

Typeset by Ben Cracknell Studios

Printed in Great Britain by Martins the Printers Ltd.,
Berwick-upon-Tweed

Contents

Acknowledgements

I would like to thank a number of people who have helped in the production of this book, in particular, my wife, Margaret, and my stepmother, Iris, at the typing and proofreading stages. A thank you to my son Matthew for his invaluable and sound advice on electronic information sources is also due. Thanks also to Alison Sharman, Pauline Fulcher and Julian Beckton (library staff of the University of Lincolnshire and Humberside) for advice on the Dewey system. Finally, I should like to thank David Barker of Cassell for his encouragement and advice throughout the preparation of this book.

Preface

For a number of years I have helped students, both in this country and abroad, with dissertation and thesis preparation. In the course of this work I have always felt there was a need for more practical advice on how to research and produce a dissertation. From my experience, students often have a lot of theoretical knowledge about the processes of research, but find this difficult to put into practice when producing the final document.

I hope the advice given in this book helps students succeed in the production of a good dissertation. I have taken a 'tips and techniques' approach, rather than concentrate on academic and pedagogical issues, which I feel are not needed at undergraduate level. A lot of the material used in this book has developed as a result of running workshops for students and I thank them for their participation and interest.

Brian White
March 1999

1 What this book is about

Introduction

Most undergraduate business and management degree students, in their final year, are required to complete a long piece of independent work. This is known by various names such as project, long essay, thesis, extended essay or dissertation. For most students it forms an important part of the final year, and is a substantial part of their total assessment. At some universities the dissertation (this is the term that will be used throughout this book) is the key factor which influences the student's final degree classification. It can determine whether you receive a first class, second class or third class degree. It makes good sense, therefore, to approach your dissertation in a positive way and regard it as a challenge. Look on it as an opportunity to demonstrate how good you are because it provides a way to produce a piece of work that sets you apart from the other students. However, the thought of having to write a 10,000–12,000 word dissertation (at some universities the length can be up to 20,000 words) often causes even the most able undergraduate student to feel undue apprehension and anxiety. In fact, the first word which comes to mind for many students when faced with the task of starting a dissertation is *HELP!*

This book has been written to provide the positive and practical help you need. It covers all the main stages you go through when preparing a dissertation and includes topics such as:

- choosing an area to study and deciding on the title;
- deciding what is research and how it is applied to business and management;
- writing a research proposal;
- selecting the best methodology to use;
- using libraries and collecting information;
- collecting your own information and data;

- evaluating and analysing the information and data you collect;
- writing up the dissertation and choosing the layout;
- working with your supervisor;
- the assessment of dissertations.

In addition, certain basic questions like 'What is a dissertation?' and 'What is the value of a dissertation?' are answered, together with advice about the necessary skills. Consideration is given to the ethical issues you may need to think about with some business and management research topics and, at the end, an annotated bibliography is included in case you should need extra help in a particular area.

Although the book takes you through the stages of preparing and writing a dissertation it does not cover the administrative and organizational requirements of individual universities. Each university should provide this sort of detail in course handbooks, via notice-boards, e-mail, etc. Most business degree programmes have course leaders, year tutors or dissertation supervisors who provide information about hand-in dates, regulations and other information about your course.

How to use this book

Quickly scan the whole book and get an overall impression of what dissertations are about. After reading it, go back to the beginning and start to work through it, chapter by chapter. When you actually begin your dissertation keep the book handy and use it as a guide.

What is a dissertation?

Let's start by asking the very basic but important question. What is a dissertation? It is not an essay; nor is it an ordinary business, management, consultancy or market research report. So what is it?

Different authors provide varying definitions, but for our purpose a dissertation can be defined as a long piece of academic writing, divided into headed sections or chapters, which researches, in detail, a particular business or management subject. This you will normally choose yourself. On your own, you will investigate areas which, in some respects, may be entirely new and unfamiliar to you. You will be expected to critique your work with that of other researchers and discuss the various theories involved. To do this successfully you will need to collect a lot of information. You will use libraries and, depending on your topic, may carry out your own research to collect new material. Having collected the information and data, you then have to interpret what it all means, and write it up in an accepted academic format. The final dissertation must demonstrate originality and evidence of academic criticism and analysis.

Not surprisingly, even the most able student can find the dissertation a daunting experience. Don't be put off. A dissertation provides you with a unique opportunity to demonstrate your academic skills. It gives you the chance to study in some detail a subject in which you have a genuine interest, and this in itself can give a great sense of personal satisfaction. It does mean, however, that you must have effective study and research skills. Before the skills you need are discussed it may help to explain the characteristic features of a dissertation. This will give you a better idea of exactly what is involved.

The characteristic features of a dissertation

- *A dissertation is an independent piece of work.* Although all your assignments on your course are independent pieces of work, in that you do them on your own and without plagiarism, a dissertation is truly independent because no other student is working on the same title. With other assignments many students may be working on the same title. This means that a dissertation gives you a chance to show how good you really are. A dissertation is an excellent indicator of a student's true ability, and can help with your final degree classification. A good dissertation mark will often help a borderline student get a higher class of degree. This point is discussed later.

- *A dissertation shows detailed knowledge and understanding.* Dissertations require a lot of information – facts and figures are needed. This means you have to spend a long time collecting and searching out relevant material. You need to demonstrate a thorough knowledge of the literature and be able to discuss the theoretical concepts of the topic.

- *A dissertation needs organization and good planning.* Because a dissertation is long, it takes time to complete and you need to be able to organize and plan the work over an extended period, sometimes between 6 and 9 months. Your ability to plan work independently over such a long period again demonstrates why dissertations are often included in courses. It shows that you can be responsible for your own learning.

- *A dissertation shows critical and analytical thinking.* Too many dissertations are spoilt because students simply describe situations. You must be prepared to question, identify trends and provide evidence to support your ideas. You have to relate theory to practice. If you have carried out research, you must defend your research design and data collection techniques. In summary, you must subject your work and that of others to serious questioning, rather than just accepting it at face value.

- *A dissertation illustrates the context of existing knowledge.* It is important that a literature review is included that collates previously published work in the same field. Your dissertation is not an isolated investigation. You need to show how it relates to what other people have done. Again, other people's work must not simply be described. It is the relationship between your work and theirs which demonstrates criticism and analysis.

- *A dissertation has a high standard of communication and presentation.* Good English, correct spelling and grammar are essential. Moreover, the work must look neat on the page. Sloppy, untidy and inaccurate work can make a dissertation fail. A dissertation must also be prepared according to an accepted format, so check your course regulations.

- *A dissertation demonstrates original work and research.* Students often think that their work must be as original as Einstein's theory of relativity. Unfortunately, very few of us have the flair and intellect of Einstein. By original work and research, we mean that you should put forward your own ideas and back them up with appropriate evidence. This might be generated as a result of a questionnaire or interview. Alternatively, you might use published information and present it in a different and new manner, which in itself is original. The emphasis again is on critical and analytical thinking; a description of either your own or other people's work without some analysis is not enough.

- *A dissertation has an academic approach.* A dissertation is an academic document and must have an appropriate format following accepted traditions of referencing styles. It should always include a bibliography. Normally it is written in a very formal style using the third person.

Value of a dissertation

Academic value

For many students the dissertation is the first independent piece of work they complete. Although all your degree work should be your own in terms of academic integrity and the absence of plagiarism, with the present-day emphasis on group work and everyone in large classes doing the same assignments, students get few chances to work completely on their own. The value of a dissertation is that it allows you to demonstrate, in a very positive way, that you can work alone. It gives you, the student, an opportunity to show your true worth.

The dissertation is an important part of the final year of your degree. On some courses the dissertation can contribute up to 20% of your assessment, and many lecturers would argue that it reflects, more than anything else you do on a course, your true intellectual ability. Certainly, it often gives a clear indication of the degree classification the student should be awarded. Imagine, as a lecturer, you are sitting in an examination board and a student's degree classification, based on four pieces of assessed work and the dissertation, is being decided. The student has one piece of work with an upper second class mark (e.g. 61%) and three pieces with lower second class marks (e.g. 58%, 58% and 59%). This student is borderline, so what final degree class would the student be given? In most cases the board would look at the dissertation mark, and if this was well in the upper second category (e.g. 67%), the chances are that the student would be given an upper second class degree. Conversely, if the mark was in the low fifties (e.g. 53%), the student would, most likely, be given a lower second class degree.

Personal and career value

In addition to being of academic importance, dissertations help with your personal and career development. As the dissertation comes towards the end of a degree programme it assesses a whole range of skills and competencies. The process of producing and writing a dissertation develops some very important skills that potential employers always require. These are termed 'personal transferable skills' and include things like planning, organizing, analysing, criticizing, information gathering, identifying and solving problems, logical thinking, time management, data interpretation, research methods, and communication skills like writing. A dissertation is something you can take with you to an interview to show to a prospective employer. It indicates that you can work independently to produce a substantial piece of work. In summary, it is piece of tangible evidence of the sort of work of which you are capable.

Producing a dissertation – the stages involved

There are a number of stages involved in the production of a dissertation and these are summarized in Figure 1.1. In reality, once you start a dissertation several things seem to happen at once – you may be designing a questionnaire, reading some recent articles, waiting for an inter-library loan order, seeing your supervisor, and so on. Good and effective time management and organization skills are essential.

Depending on your topic, the time spent on each stage will vary. Many students begin their work towards the end of their second year by producing a dissertation proposal. If possible, follow this up over the summer vacation by conducting the literature search and working out any methodological issues. Remember there may be other assignments in your final year as well as the dissertation. The way you plan your work should take into account your complete workload. The ideal situation, depending on your submission dates, would be to have most of the data collection for the dissertation complete by December/ January in your final year. This should ensure enough time to analyse the information and complete the writing up and presentation for the hand-in later in the year.

The skills you need

It is important to remember that a good dissertation is not written overnight. It takes time, considerable planning and effort. Mention has already been made of some of the intellectual and practical skills needed and these are further discussed below.

- *Library and information retrieval skills* (see Chapter 7). Dissertations require a great deal of information so be sure you know how to use libraries to search for the material you need. Be aware of the information services (e.g. inter-library loans) that may be available. Keep detailed citation records of everything you read. Either use cards or set up a computer database. Associated with the collection of library material is the way you use and evaluate it to inform the literature review and the overall research design of the dissertation. See details of exactly what to record on pages 143–5.

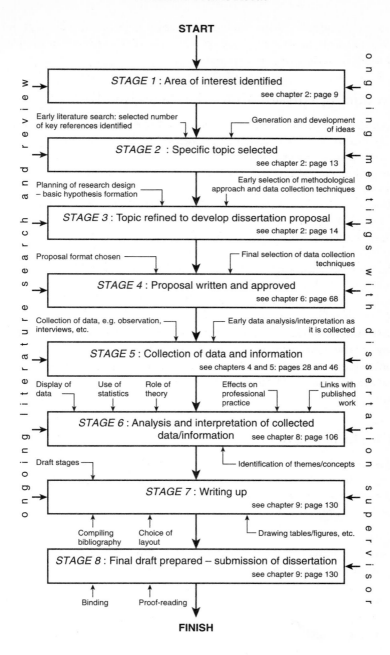

Figure 1.1 The stages involved in producing a dissertation

- *Writing and note-taking skills* (see Chapter 9). Dissertations involve a lot of writing. Before you start, decide on the required format and the method of acknowledging and referencing other people's work. Decide how to lay out the bibliography of the finished dissertation. Certain universities provide style manuals and handbooks – always follow their advice. When making notes, be sure you are doing just that and not simply copying out large chunks of text. You will only have to sort it out later. You may as well do it at the start.

- *Research skills* (see Chapters 4 and 5). Dissertations need new information and data. The approach you take and the methods you select to collect information are as important as the material you collect. A sound methodology explained with reasons gives your work credibility. It means the results collected and conclusions arrived at are more valid and academically sound. Research skills also include data handling and interpretation. If you think you are going to need, and use, special software packages like SPSS, NUDIST, etc., practise using them early.

- *Personal skills*. These include self-motivation, self-discipline, time management, and the ability to plan and organize. In short, these skills are all about being independent and taking responsibility for you own work and decisions.

A final word

Hopefully by now you will have a good idea of what dissertations are all about and the processes involved in producing one. The rest of the book gives more advice with respect to the different stages concerned.

2   Choosing and developing a subject to investigate

Introduction

This chapter looks at the mechanics and processes of completing a dissertation. In particular, it will focus on two aspects: the choice of a topic to study, and how that topic may be refined and developed to form a framework for the dissertation. The proposal is then written which covers in some detail exactly what you want to do. From experience, the initial choice of subject often causes students a great deal of concern and seems to present a lot of problems. As highlighted earlier, the dissertation is possibly the most important piece of written work that you undertake in your final year. It is essential to choose a subject that you can handle with confidence and interest. In fact, the correct choice of subject is the first step towards a successful dissertation.

In the early stages don't worry about the exact wording of a title for the dissertation as this can be finalized later. The initial emphasis should be on selecting the general area and seeing if it is suitable (via some of the techniques described below) to develop into a proposal.

This chapter, therefore, considers a number of issues which are all inter-related. Don't consider each in isolation: always relate one to another to get the overall picture.

The issues discussed include:

- a discussion of the factors which may influence your choice;
- a list of sources you can use to generate early ideas;
- a summary of the techniques you can use to establish the parameters of the dissertation.

Factors which may influence your choice of subject

There are a number of factors which may influence the choice of a dissertation topic. It may be an interest, something connected with work, or something else. Read through the following, noting the points which apply to you.

- *Am I going to be genuinely interested in the topic?* A real interest in a subject is vitally important. It helps when the going gets tough, and that will definitely happen. With even the brightest student, there often comes a point in a dissertation when everything seems out of place and things do not go to plan. A real interest and commitment keep you motivated; energy and enthusiasm are essential ingredients for a successful dissertation. To give an example, two students recently produced good dissertations by linking them with their hobbies. One student was extremely keen on fashion and wrote on the rise and interest of 'modern designer labels'. The other, with a passion for football, researched the issue of 'football sponsorship' by large multinational companies.

- *Do I already know a lot about a topic?* You may already have a lot of information about a subject which could form the basis of a dissertation. For example, you may have collected a lot of material for a previous assignment which you never used. Why not use it now if you can?

- *Is it a well-trodden area?* Don't be afraid to choose a subject that is popular. For example, the management of change and business process re-engineering are current business issues. This means there is a great deal of information available. A lot of information does mean, however, that when searching through material you need to be really focused and know exactly the sort of thing you are looking for. You must also attempt to make your treatment of the topic different – don't simply repeat a piece of research unless there is a good and valid reason.

- *Can I cope with the topic in terms of depth and breadth?* Dissertations need to demonstrate appropriate academic rigour and depth: for example, some topics may need quantitative methods which could require a good level of mathematical ability. It is important to match the topic with your proven academic strengths and skills, so if quantitative methods and statistics are a problem, choose an area that does not require advanced mathematical skills. If you are good at talking to people and can empathize with their views, then go for the interview and similar techniques. There are, however, certain skills that all students need and these include good library and writing skills.

- *Are the resources, e.g. time, facilities, money, equipment, etc. available?* It is important that any topic selected can be completed on time. Don't be over-ambitious; ensure that the final choice is feasible and manageable in the time available. Plan the work realistically, especially when deciding on the methodology. It takes time, for example, to run several focus groups, conduct interviews and record observations. Research costs money and with most dissertations it's the student who pays. You may decide you want to conduct a postal questionnaire, but can you afford the cost of postage? If you need to interview certain people, have you got the time and the money to do so? The resource factor should never be overlooked. With commercial research it is often the money which governs the type and scale of the final investigation.

- *Availability of information.* Dissertations need a lot of information; they require you to search out and assess the literature that is already published in the area. The literature has to be reviewed and this forms the background for your work. Literature is so important that a separate chapter is devoted to it (see Chapter 7). Availability of material should be a key factor when you make the final choice, and an early visit to the library, once an idea is identified, is essential. Be practical and realistic and if little or no material is in stock or easily retrieved by, for example, inter-library loans, then you may be well advised to start again. A dissertation has to be completed within a fixed length of time. You haven't the luxury of an unlimited time span to work on a topic on which little has been published. Always check before you finally decide on a subject that there is adequate information available.

- *Is the topic appropriate to my degree?* The topics of business and management are wide in scope, covering almost anything 'from a pin to an elephant'. A pin company faces the same problems of finance, human resource management, marketing, operations, etc. as any other company. Elephants are found in zoos which are run as independent organizations and also face similar problems. This gives enormous scope when selecting a topic to study. You can give almost anything a business and management flavour. However, there is a catch and, with certain topics, it is very easy to lose the business focus. The following three real-life examples will hopefully explain what can easily happen.

  1. In recent years UK farmers have been encouraged to set aside part of their land for recreation and other non-agricultural

purposes. The scheme when introduced was called 'set aside'. The dissertation's aim was to investigate the strategic management implications of the scheme. The student working on it became so interested in the way the land was used that the dissertation started to fit more closely with an environmental studies degree.

2. A second student was interested to see if a proposed by-pass around St Helen's, Lancashire, would influence the economy of the town. The student became so engrossed with the planning and construction of the by-pass that the work was more relevant to a civil engineering and building degree.

3. The final example concerns a student looking at management practices associated with factory farming. The student's focus wavered and the research became more concerned with ethical and animal rights issues. Although the work was good, it was not appropriate to a degree in business studies. With controversial topics like this, it is imperative that you keep a sense of balance. It is a characteristic of academic work that any opinion, however contentious, should always be based on evidence taken from either the literature or empirical research.

Fortunately, with all three students their supervisors picked up the loss of direction very early on and excellent dissertations were produced. Always keep the main objectives in mind and guard against veering off-track.

- *Is the topic relevant to my needs?* Many students by the time they reach the final year have a career choice in mind. Why not, therefore, centre your dissertation around it? If you want to work in marketing, it makes sense to select a marketing topic. You can use your dissertation to help you build a CV and, as stated earlier, the completed work is something to take along to an interview. Even if it isn't finished it will at least give you something to talk about.

- *Does the topic agree with course regulations?* Always be aware of what you are supposed to produce. Certain courses set precise limits as to what can be done and the range of subjects that can be studied. Some courses even give provisional titles. If in doubt see the course leader early and if you are allocated a dissertation supervisor (see Chapter 10) have a talk as soon as possible. Follow their advice and use their experience.

Generating dissertation ideas – sources to use

So far we have worked through the factors that can influence your choice of subject, but you still need to choose the subject in the first place. The following may help you generate the initial idea.

- *Reading business and management literature.* Looking through new books and recent editions of journals may help. Recent publications reflect current trends and ideas in a subject; these are things which are happening *now*. There may be a number of subjects which you find interesting. Make a note of them, and using some of the techniques described in the next section, decide whether they can form the framework for a dissertation. From experience it is best to concentrate on articles found in journals. Journal titles vary from the very general (e.g. *The Economist*) to the more specialized (e.g. *Journal of Management Studies*). All are good and may help you come up with an idea.

- *I'd like to know more about that.* Has there been anything on your course so far when you have thought to yourself 'That's interesting, I'd like to know more about that'? Often topics like this can be developed into a dissertation. Also you can re-use material collected for a previous assignment which you found especially interesting.

- *Current events and using the media e.g. TV, press, radio.* Events like big company take-overs often hit the headlines and such current events can sometimes be used to develop good dissertations. The government might announce new initiatives for industry which could become a starting point. In the world of business and management you must look out for, and be aware of, relevant contemporary issues. Newspapers like the *Financial Times* report recent events and can be a source of ideas. Many Sunday papers have special business supplements that are worth looking through. There are also a number of current affairs, documentary and news programmes about business (e.g. *The Money Programme, Panorama, Newsnight,* etc.) which may contain items that can form the basis of a dissertation.

- *Work experience.* Many undergraduate business students, as part of their course, spend time away from the university in industry, on what is termed 'placement'. On some courses this can be as long as one year. You may be a part-time student and can use your job as a starting point for a dissertation, or you may have had a vacation job which can be used. In fact, any time spent in a commercial and external organization can often generate an idea. There may be a problem in the company that needs researching which can be the start of a dissertation. One example was a student working in a well-established and respected, but traditional family-run, bleaching and dyeing company. The company was interested in investing in new technology and this formed the idea for what turned out to be an excellent dissertation. However, if you have worked in a company and would like to use them as a basis for a dissertation it is essential to obtain their written permission. When working in an organization you may see confidential information which the company wishes to remain unpublished. Although it may be good material to use in a dissertation, you cannot use it. A word of caution when using real-life examples: companies often expect the student to produce a type of consultancy report. A dissertation and a consultancy report are not the same thing. A report pays more attention to final recommendations and results, whereas the dissertation requires the literature to be reviewed in detail and the methodology carefully worked out. Moreover, a dissertation relates academic theory and practice to the topic being researched – again, this is usually absent in a consultancy report.

Developing the idea – some techniques to try

Selecting the general topic is only the start. It now needs to be refined and developed in order to determine if it can be expanded into a dissertation. You are going to take your original idea and see how it may be broken down into smaller, discrete areas. These can then be re-arranged and structured into a logical sequence to form the framework of the dissertation. In other words, you have to draw up an initial dissertation outline that will form the basis for the proposal (see Chapter 6).

However, don't be too ambitious – you only have a limited amount of time to complete a dissertation. It's not going to be your life's work. A criticism levelled by many external examiners is that many undergraduate business dissertations are too wide and unfocused; they lack direction. It is far better to study a small topic in considerable detail than attempt a broad subject which, because of its complexity, only allows you to achieve a superficial level of analysis.

At this development stage you are trying to generate a series of research questions (sometimes called research objectives). Ask yourself, for each area identified, questions like 'What do I want to find out?', 'Which research methods would be the best to use?', and 'How can this topic be investigated and researched?'

In summary, take your early idea and divide it up into smaller ideas. Look at each small idea in turn and decide if it's worth keeping. If it is, then decide the best method(s) to use to research it, in order to make it part of a larger piece of work. You are trying to determine the precise focus of the study and a list of areas which, in turn, will be examined, together with the ways in which you intend to examine them.

At this early stage go to the library and carry out an initial literature search to identify how much information is available. At the start there isn't the time to read everything you find, but keep a full record of all items you discover. Attempt to trace about ten recent review articles, which together should provide the current state of knowledge on the subject. These should give enough background on which to base the dissertation. Once the dissertation is in full swing, then the full literature search can begin.

If this early visit to the library identifies only a very small number of references, seriously consider abandoning the original topic and starting again. You must have a fair amount of previous published work from which to start so you can review the literature and relate your intended research to established theory. As stated earlier, availability of information is a key factor in determining the success of a dissertation. If the visit to the library is unsuccessful, then discuss the whole issue with your supervisor and follow their advice.

Established researchers have experience to fall back on to help them to take an initial idea and build it into a more structured outline. If you are uncertain how to go about this, then a number of techniques can be used to develop the initial idea and these are described in the next section. Give all of them a try and see which you prefer. Each one also helps you produce a 'shopping list' of things to look for when you start your literature search in the library. During the early stages give some thought to drawing up a provisional timetable. Estimate how much time you think each part may take. It is very easy to spend too much time on one area and then have to rush the writing up, for example.

Here are some basic techniques to help you develop your initial idea.

- *Brainstorming.* This is still one of the best ways to come up with original ideas and is very popular in business. Although often used in groups, it can be done alone. It is very similar to 'mind mapping'. Simply write all your ideas down on a sheet of paper. Use a big sheet if possible. When you run out of ideas go back and review each one in turn, deleting those which you feel are unsuitable. It is also helpful to think how you would go about researching each one. When the remaining ideas are arranged in a logical order you normally have a good outline for a dissertation. Figure 2.1 shows a brainstorm plan for a dissertation on the use of bar codes and the retail industry.

- *The 'Post-it' pad technique.* This method uses a pad of 'Post-it' notes. If you prefer, you can use small sheets of either card or paper. It's like brainstorming in that you write down all the ideas which come to mind – one idea on each sheet of paper. At the end spread all the pieces in front of you and arrange them in a logical order, rejecting those that really seem out of place. The advantage over brainstorming is that as you move the papers around you tend to spark off new thoughts and suggestions, and these can be added to the pile of notes. Finally, copy onto a fresh sheet of paper your final list of research objectives. Some researchers call this method 'cluster analysis'. Don't confuse it with the statistical term 'cluster sampling'; the two are not the same.

- *Question time approach.* Often the above techniques become untidy, and for the really meticulous person asking simple straightforward questions may be enough to trigger the imagination. Questions like Who?, What?, Where?, When?, How?, and Why? will suffice. Make the questions as focused as possible and decide exactly what you want to find out. Ask questions about the type of information needed and the best research methods to use to investigate each idea identified.

- *Concepts, trends, implications and issues.* This is very much like the question time approach, but you start with a series of general questions such as: Are there any economic concepts, trends, implications and issues involved? Are there any technological concepts, trends, implications and issues involved? Are there any legal concepts, trends, implications and issues involved? Are there any social concepts, trends, implications and issues involved? From these general questions you can delve more deeply and again come up with a number of more focused issues on your original idea.

In addition to the above, a number of other techniques are available, e.g. fish bone diagrams and relevance trees, that work just as well. All

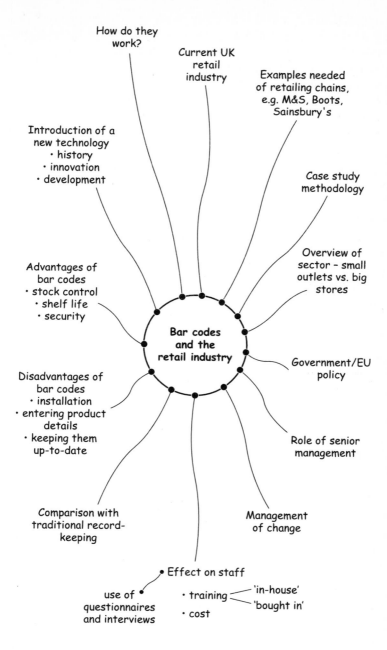

Figure 2.1 Brainstorm plan for the dissertation 'An investigation into the impact of bar codes on the retail industry'

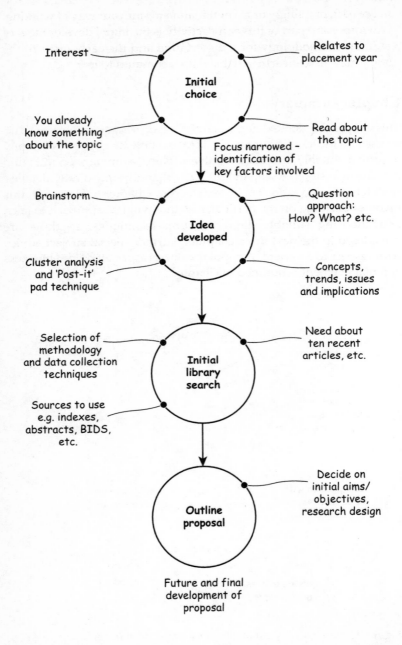

Figure 2.2 A suggested scheme to develop a dissertation topic

of them are simple and, when used correctly, can be very effective. You can use each one singly or in combination to suit your way of working.

An important part of this early activity is the initial development of a suitable methodology for a dissertation and the early visits to the library may also unearth suitable data techniques to use.

Chapter summary

This chapter has looked at the start of the dissertation process. It has focused on the identification of an idea and how that can be developed to form a suitable dissertation subject. This is summarized in Figure 2.2. The next step is to expand the early thoughts into a fully detailed research proposal and this is described in Chapter 6. However, this involves deciding on the particular methodological approach to take, and choosing suitable data collection techniques, so these are considered in the next three chapters. Further special subject advice with respect to a variety of popular subjects associated with business and management is outlined in Chapter 11.

3 What research is and choosing an appropriate methodology

Introduction

So far this book has explained what is meant by the term dissertation and the things you need to think about when starting one. Advice has been given about choosing and developing a suitable topic to study. Mention has been made of the importance of research and the practical considerations which need to be borne in mind. Care also needs to be taken not only in choosing a topic to study, but in deciding how to study it. The selection of an appropriate methodology and the choice of suitable techniques are of paramount importance. This chapter considers some very basic issues. These include what is meant by research and how this relates to business and management, and also whether particular methodological approaches are more suitable and reliable than others. The importance of research design is discussed, along with a consideration of ethical issues in research.

Methodology and methods

The approach a researcher uses to investigate a subject is termed the *methodology*. Methodology refers to the philosophical basis on which the research is founded. The particular techniques used to collect data and information are termed *methods*. Don't become confused by the terms 'methodology' and 'method' – the two are not the same.

Each academic discipline, over time, has developed characteristic methodologies and methods. A scientist, for example, designs and carries out experiments, a sociologist uses surveys, and a historian examines old documents and records. Business studies, by its very nature, is wide-ranging. It is a general subject and covers many areas. It therefore employs a variety of methodologies and methods. What is important is that for your dissertation a recognized and accepted methodology, together with accurate methods of data collection, is used. This means the information you collect is more reliable and valid. Although there are many established ways of approaching a problem and collecting material, don't be afraid to try new ways of research. You must, of course, provide a thorough and well-thought-out rationale to back up any new idea.

What is research?

Before the different approaches and techniques are explained, it is important to address a very basic question. What is research? Academics who study the philosophy of research consider this question at some length and in some detail. This is not the intention here; the aim is to give you a basic understanding so that you think seriously about how you intend to investigate your selected topic.

Different academics define research in different ways. An easy to understand explanation is that given by Johnson (1994). She defines research as 'A focused and systematic enquiry that goes beyond generally available knowledge to acquire specialised and detailed information, providing a basis for analysis and elucidatory comment on the topic of enquiry.'

Johnson (1994) highlights four key issues in this definition:

1. *Research should be focused, not general.* For example, if you were investigating the role of total quality management (TQM) and its importance for industry, would it be better to look at all industries (e.g. marketing, leisure, manufacturing, etc.) or one in great detail? This means that when you begin a piece of research you need to set up precise research questions to decide exactly what you want to do.

2. *Systematic – the approach to a problem should be structured and organized.* Take the above example with respect to a particular manufacturing company. Would you ask every employee you came across in the company what they thought about TQM or would it be better first to think about the issues associated with TQM and arrive at a series of structured questions? You could then put the same set of questions to a selected number of people in the company. To arrive at the questions you would need to find out what other people had written about TQM and how this may be related to manufacturing. This would involve collecting information already available. You would then collect and

evaluate your own data and compare it with existing material. This would be a synthesis of the new material with the old.

3. *Beyond generally available knowledge.* Carrying out research implies that you add to present knowledge. After completing the work on TQM you should know more about the concept and have a greater insight into its issues and problems. This in turn may generate more research ideas which need to be resolved and studied further.

4. *A basis for analysis and elucidatory comments.* After having carried out research you should be able to arrive at some conclusions which may agree or disagree with current accepted theory and understanding about TQM and the manufacturing industry. Either way, you would need to provide a reasoned account to support your case. If your work was limited to one manufacturing company, you would need to consider how your results related to the manufacturing industry as a whole. It may even be possible to make tentative conclusions about TQM and all industry.

In summary, research involves finding out about things, but in a structured way. If you were about to buy a new computer, car, hi-fi, or house, you would look around, compare prices, after-sales service, and so on. You might look at specialist magazines, watch a consumer programme on TV, etc. In other words, before you bought anything you would collect evidence and evaluate it before making a final decision. The same procedure applies to writing a dissertation.

Research and business practice

It is essential to relate how the meaning of research applies to the world of business, and if there is anything special about it. Easterby-Smith, Thorpe and Lowe (1991) regard management research as distinctive. They argue it is eclectic, i.e. wide-ranging, and crosses many subject boundaries. It is, therefore, difficult to centre any research in one particular discipline.

Moreover, as a consequence of research, business and management professional practice is often changed and improved. Research is not always carried out for research's sake. In a discipline such as chemistry, research, although important, often simply adds to the body of knowledge of the subject. The research itself, unless it results in new techniques, does not always bring about any change in the way chemists work. In management, however, the results of research often change the way managers act and carry out their daily work. Imagine research has been carried out into the way senior executives greet their staff first thing in the morning, and it was found that a handshake improved productivity and profits. The chances are that all executives would make the point of shaking the hands of their employees as often as possible. The behaviour of the executives, therefore, would have been influenced by the research. This example is somewhat simple, but in business and management, research is often related to professional practice.

Senior managers and executives are powerful people and usually difficult to contact. They have influence over their employees' lives in terms of job security, pay and conditions. The researcher may face problems gaining access to executives. If access is achieved, and the research completed, what happens if the findings are controversial? Business research can put the researcher in a vulnerable position, especially if they are part of the company being researched.

Finally, all organizations deal with confidential and commercial issues. Access to these by the researcher may be difficult and, if it is allowed, it might not be possible to publish the research in the public domain. There are ethical issues here which, depending on the topic, may compromise the researcher and other people concerned. This again makes research in business and management somewhat different.

The research process – different schools of thought

Research is a process, a series of activities unfolding over time. It involves a number of things such as choice of the research design, the collection of data, the evaluation of results, and so on. One of the most important decisions to make is the general approach the research is going to take. There are different schools of thought on this. As identified above, academics spend a great deal of time discussing the philosophy of research and research design. A lengthy account here is unnecessary, but a basic understanding will help to clarify your choice of methodology and research design. It will help you decide which approach is best in a particular situation. It may even assist if you need either to create a new methodology or modify an existing one.

A criticism made by many examiners about business dissertations is that the research methodology lacks clarity and direction. In many instances the method of data collection is not well thought out or suitable to the subject being investigated. Often at the early stages students become impatient and simply want to chase results and information. Remember, how you collect evidence is as important as the evidence itself. If your results are to be believed, then the way you collect them in the first place must also be believable.

Let's consider some of the basic methodological choices, noting that each approach has different advantages and limitations. Methodology is concerned with how the researcher views the world in which he or she carries out the research. Suppose you are a member of a group, and are researching how that group reacts in different situations. It could be argued that as a group member, it would be very difficult to stand back and be truly objective about the way you study the group's activity. On the other hand, it could be argued that, with suitable techniques, it is possible to stand back and take an objective view on how to research the group.

In the main, therefore, academics distinguish two main areas: *quantitative* research and *qualitative* research. Quantitative research involves an objective way of studying things, whereas a qualitative approach assumes that this is difficult and the research is subjective.

Quantitative research, sometimes referred to as *positivist*, is scientific in approach. It aims to be objective and collects and uses numerical data. Qualitative research takes the view that it is very difficult for researchers to stand back and be objective, since they are really part of the process being researched. This type of research is sometimes called *relativist* or *phenomenalist*. Academics argue about the merits and limitations of each approach and, sometimes, even what each term really means. As far as your dissertation is concerned, adopt the methodology that best suits your background, interest and, most importantly, the subject you are investigating. The various methods of data collection associated with each approach are described in Chapter 4 and Chapter 5. At this point the two methodologies are explained in outline only.

Quantitative research

With this type of research the results are given numerical values and the researcher uses a mathematical and statistical treatment to help evaluate the results. Scientists carrying out experiments use this approach. Surveys by marketing people, using questionnaires and interviews where responses are given numerical values, would also be described as quantitative research.

Qualitative research

With this approach data is usually collected in the form of descriptions. Even though some of the methods used, such as interviews, are used in quantitative research, the difference is that qualitative researchers only use non-mathematical procedures when interpreting and explaining their research. In management and business this approach is used to study the way organizations, groups and individuals behave and interact.

Is it possible to combine qualitative and quantitative research?
It certainly is. You might decide to carry out a survey after investigating a subject from a qualitative perspective. For example, after studying certain changes in an organization, you may decide to survey, by questionnaire, opinions (e.g. those of managers, administrative staff, clients, etc.) about a particular aspect associated with the change. Looking at the same problem from a number of viewpoints is an excellent way to verify your interpretation and conclusions. Using a number of different approaches is termed *triangulation*. This is referred to later after the various methods of data collection have been explained (see pages 66–7).

Research design

Research design is a general term that covers a number of separate, but related, issues associated with your research. It includes the aims of the research, the final selection of the appropriate methodology, the data collection techniques you intend to use, the chosen methods of data analysis and interpretation, and how all this fits in with the literature. Figure 3.1 attempts to link all these issues together.

Two important concepts to build into the design are validity and reliability. Validity is concerned with the idea that the research design fully addresses the research questions and objectives you are trying to answer and achieve. This implies that as much planning as possible must be done beforehand. Reliability is about consistency and research, and whether another researcher could use your design and obtain similar findings. This does not imply that their interpretation and conclusions will be the same. The chances are that they will be different, since this is where the judgement of individual researchers comes into play.

Overall, the research design is the blueprint or detailed outline for the whole of your research and dissertation. It relies on careful forward planning.

Ethical considerations and research

It may help to start by explaining what is meant by ethics. As you can imagine, many academics have written a great deal about it, and one of the most straightforward definitions of ethics is that of Churchill (1995): 'moral principles and values that govern the way an individual or group conducts its activities'.

Business research comes into direct contact with people either on their own, or when they are part of a larger group, such as in a company or an organization. Moreover, much of the research is qualitative in approach, and the outcome of the research can be subject to wide interpretation. As such, the biases, intent and views of everyone concerned with a piece of research are open to debate. There are occasions, therefore, when the researcher (in this case you) needs an appreciation of the ethical issues which may be involved at all stages of the research.

Nowadays many universities pay particular attention to ethical and associated issues and have codes of practice which both staff and students are expected to follow. A number of professional bodies (e.g. the British Sociological Association) produce guidelines with respect to the conduct of research. As a researcher it is your responsibility to ensure that you follow any prescribed codes where they are applicable.

If you are not provided with any set guidelines or code of practice, the following may help when carrying out the work:

- Only involve people with their consent or knowledge. Participants should always have enough information about the research to make an informed decision as to whether to take part or not. During the research participants should retain the right to draw back and remove consent if they so wish.
- Never coerce or persuade people to participate in research. Participants have the right to choose for themselves whether to be the subjects of your research.
- Never withhold information on the true nature of the research. Explain to all concerned what it's all about.
- Tell the truth about the research and never deceive participants in any way.
- Never induce participants to do things which could destroy their self-confidence or self-determination.
- Never expose people to situations which could cause mental or physical stress.
- Respect a participant's right to privacy. If anonymity and confidentiality are guaranteed, this should always be maintained.
- Treat all groups in the same research project alike, with consideration and respect.

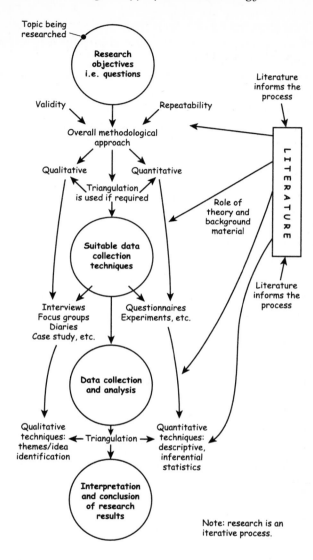

Figure 3.1 A summary of the features of research design

Finally, when you write up your research, you should present the evidence with honesty and integrity and never knowingly allow anyone to misuse or misinterpret your work. People who have taken part in the research also have a right to know about the results of the research, unless there are very valid reasons to the contrary.

4   Techniques of qualitative research, including case study and action research

Introduction

The previous chapter explained what is meant by research and briefly discussed the differences between qualitative and quantitative research. This chapter focuses specifically on qualitative methodology and explains some of its data collection techniques.

Qualitative research is a staple form of research of the social sciences, politics and economics, all subjects closely linked with business. It is a descriptive, non-numerical way to collect and interpret information. Researchers who support this approach argue that no two situations are the same and every phenomenon is unique. The research cannot, therefore, be measured in the conventional sense, since it takes place in actual and everyday settings, not in a laboratory. It investigates the way people react, work, live and manage their daily lives.

The researcher is often part of the research being carried out, which further complicates the situation. For example, a student on industrial placement investigating some aspect of a company is part of that company. It could be claimed that the student is too involved to stand back and be truly objective (i.e., positivist). With a qualitative investigation the researcher observes a great deal and any results are mostly descriptive in nature rather than sets of numerical data. Over the years a number of different qualitative techniques have evolved. Some of the better known ones are explained in this chapter.

They include *interviews*, *observation* and the use of *diaries*. *Case study* and *action research* are also included. Strictly speaking, case studies and action research are not discrete qualitative techniques. They are better described as research strategies and each employs a number of different methods (sometimes quantitative ones). In the main, however, they use more description, both in the collection and interpretation of data, and for this reason have been included in this chapter.

The list of methods below is not definitive and the annotated bibliography (Chapter 12) should help if you need more information. Whether you adopt a qualitative or quantitative methodology, or a combination of both, remember you are not expected to use every technique going. What is essential is that the final choice is relevant and workable with your particular topic. Moreover, be aware of the advantages and limitations involved and be able to provide a rationale for the final selection. The reasoning behind the choice is never wasted, as it is written up and included in the methodology section of the final dissertation.

Interviews

An interview is a popular form of data collection and can provide, when properly conducted, a rich source of material.

Advantages of interviews

They can be used in a variety of contexts and situations, and in conjunction with other research methods. For example, a preliminary interview may identify problems which can either be incorporated into a questionnaire or form the basis of a later and more searching interview. The type of interview will depend on the nature of information you want to collect, and it may range from a highly structured predesigned list of questions to a free-ranging conversation. The real benefit of an interview is that you are face-to-face with the interviewee, so you can clear up any misunderstandings immediately. Either side can question what they do not understand. Also, during the interview the researcher can re-word or re-order the questions if something unexpected happens.

Disadvantages of interviews

They are very time-consuming. You need to take into account length of interview, travelling to and from interview, transcription of tapes, notes, etc. As a result, you may only interview a small sample which may not be representative of the population. You need to be sure the interview is the best way to get the information you want.

Moreover, with all interviews there are problems of bias, reliability and validity which must be addressed throughout the whole interview process. Be aware, for instance, of the interviewee who wants to please the interviewer and, as a result, may not tell the truth. The interviewer must ensure that their personal views and, as a result, bias do not creep in when the interview information is being evaluated and interpreted. The interviewer–interviewee relationship is very important and it is essential that the whole process is carefully planned. Finally, remember a friendly spontaneous chat with either a friend or group of people does not constitute an interview.

Interview preparation

The following checklist highlights the main points to think about when planning interviews.

1. Know the background well and decide if the interview technique is the best way to get the information you need. For example, details about the organization, management structure of a company, or its financial situation may be obtained from annual reports and other company literature, often already in the public domain. An interview can be used to investigate the views of the employees on how the structure works in practice and whether their opinions about it are taken on board by senior management. Thorough planning at the start is essential.

2. Decide on the type of interview you want: individual, group, telephone, structured or unstructured (sometimes termed in-depth or focused interviews). Quantitative research also uses interviews, but the respondent's answers are coded numerically and then analysed mathematically.

3. Think over how you intend to select potential interviewees. Once chosen, it is a good idea to brief them very thoroughly about the format the interview will take. Make arrangements to let them read the final dissertation if they want to. You need to develop a rapport with the people taking part. Always be honest and well-mannered and use your common sense, and this will take you a long way. Remember the people being interviewed are giving up their time and doing you a favour. Also there may be a good age gap between you as a student and the interviewee, so never patronize or show condescension.

4. Decide exactly what you want to ask. Devise, structure and order the questions for focused interviews. With more free-ranging unstructured interviews a prompt list of the topics you want to discuss is needed. It is a good idea to ask more than one question

about the same topic; this helps cross-check and correlate validity of answers. It is also a good idea to mix the form of questions. At the beginning use closed questions (i.e. ones which can be answered with a 'Yes' or a 'No') and lead up to more open questions at the end (e.g. 'What are your views on ...?'). Open questions can usually probe more sensitive areas. Remember, do not use specialized terminology or jargon, use everyday language the interviewee can understand. Consider the age of the inter-viewee. An eighty-year-old discussing working conditions may use a very different vocabulary from someone in their mid-twenties.

5. Be clear about the type of information you want. For example, is it personal background (e.g. age, marital status, education, work experience) or behavioural detail (e.g. what they did in the past, what they are doing now and what they would like to do in the future), or opinion (e.g. how do they feel about a subject?) you need? It helps to divide the questions up into topic areas. This makes the interpretation of material much easier.

6. Always pilot the final list of questions and topics on a small sample of people. This ensures the questions are clear to understand and helps remove ambiguity. A pilot session will also help you time the interview.

7. Consider how you intend to analyse the information you collect. This may influence how the questions are asked in the first place and should make the whole procedure a lot more straightforward. A look at Chapter 8 may help.

8. Choose a non-threatening environment for the interview, free from distractions and interruptions. This is not easy if you are visiting the interviewee at work.

9. Make sure all official channels are sorted out. A letter from your supervisor explaining about your course and the part played by the dissertation often resolves things like this.

10. Don't make the interview too long – tell the interviewee the estimated time and stick to it.

11. How will you record the information: tape recorder, video camcorder, notes, checklist? Only use a video or tape recorder with permission, as some people find them intimidating. Although taping ensures accuracy, transcribing tapes is time-consuming and can be expensive.

12. Finally, keep an accurate and full record of all the stages involved. This includes how you decided on the type of interview, the selection of the interviewees, choosing the questions to ask, and recording the responses – in fact you should make detailed notes on the whole process from start to finish. This can all be written up and forms an important part of the methodology section of the final dissertation.

Types of interview
Interviews either take place with individuals or groups of people.

PERSONAL INTERVIEWS
Interviews with individuals are known as personal interviews, and can either be structured or unstructured. Each will be described in turn. In a structured personal interview the interviewer has a list of prescribed questions for the interviewee. The advantage of this technique is that you can conduct a larger number of interviews, since the data collected is easier to interpret.

In unstructured personal interviews the interview takes the form of a discussion, and the interviewer directs the conversation by identifying a number of topics and allows the interviewee to talk them through in their own time. This type of interview provides a great deal of information, but the main disadvantage is often in interpreting the material collected. It can also take up more time than a structured interview so usually a smaller number of interviews is carried out. Unstructured interviews are excellent where the aim is to understand the perspective of the interviewee and the personal meanings they attach to different situations.

GROUP INTERVIEWS
In certain instances you may wish to interview a group of people about a particular topic, for example, their opinions about senior management and how decisions are made in a company. You tend to act as a prompt and direct the general discussion. Group interviews are sometimes termed *focus groups* and the interviewer is called the *moderator*. With this type of interview it is important to have a list of topics which you intend to discuss or the whole session may lose direction and become disorganized. With group interviews you need to be aware of group dynamics and ensure that one person does not take over the discussion at the expense of other members in the group. In this situation you must encourage all members of the group to respond. Questions like 'Do you agree with Matthew's opinion, Margaret?' may help Margaret

to join in. However, with group interviews you must never embarrass any member of the group or make them feel inferior or ill at ease.

There are many well-known variations of the group interview technique. These include *cognitive mapping* which is a specialized group interview that usually takes place in an action research setting. It is used a lot in strategic planning, for example, when a group of managers is faced with an issue to resolve. The *critical incident technique* is also used in interview sessions. Here the people being interviewed talk about a specific incident which they regard as critical and which may have brought about significant changes in their lives.

Carrying out the interview
When carrying out interviews the following checklist should help.

- It is important at the start to establish the nature of the relationship. Thank the interviewee(s) for agreeing to be interviewed. Explain the background and format of the interview and whether you are going to ask a series of specific questions (i.e. you are going to carry out a structured interview) or have a discussion about a series of related topics (i.e. an unstructured interview).
- It is essential at the start to confirm confidentiality and anonymity especially if there are sensitive issues involved.
- Non-verbal contact, such as nodding, facial expression, eye contact, smiling and showing interest, is important, and can often make the interviewee more at ease. You need to demonstrate empathy and even how you dress must be appropriate to the occasion.
- Confirm how long the interview will take and stick to it. If taping, ask for permission.
- At the end of the interview it is a good idea to run quickly through the answers. This helps you to sum up the main points and check on the accuracy of the answers. It may also trigger other issues the interviewee(s) may want to mention. Always allow some time at the end for any other comments the interviewee(s) would like to make.
- Finally, listen to what is said. It is the interviewee's ideas and opinions you want – you know yours!

At the end, while everything is still fresh in your memory, go over the interview to make sure you understand any notes. Write down any other comments and impressions you have; they will all help at the interpretation stage.

Observation

It could be argued that the most obvious method of data collection is observation: an accurate record of what people do and say in real-life situations. In fact, one of the most influential management gurus, Henry Mintzberg, made his reputation by writing about his observations on what senior managers did during their normal working day. Mintzberg spent a week in five middle- to large-sized organizations (a consulting firm, a technology company, a hospital, a school, and a consumer goods company) observing how the senior executive in each occupied their time. Mintzberg's book (*The Nature of Managerial Work*), published in 1973, is well worth a read on how the technique of observation can be used to best effect.

Observation is a good method to use in the area of business. It lends itself to many different situations and is popular with students on industrial placement. Correctly applied, it can be an effective method to use for the undergraduate dissertation.

The success of observation as a technique depends on a number of important factors. These include the accurate reporting and description of the topic under investigation, free access to all aspects of the investigation and plenty of time for the observations to take place.

When carrying out observation you must have a thorough background of the situation being researched. It is essential to identify exactly the sort of information you want to observe, everything from general features to specific detail. You have to record a lot of material, and this may range from what people say to one another to how they behave and what they actually do in their job. In addition, non-verbal information, for instance how they look and dress, may have a bearing on the subject being researched. Observation takes place in real-life situations, so you need to be alert to sudden changes which may influence the research.

Types of observation

There are two ways the observation can be carried out. There is *participant observation* and *non-participant observation* (sometimes termed *structured observation*). Either can be carried out with everyone knowing about the research (i.e. *overt observation*) or in secret, with no-one in the know (i.e. *covert observation*). Some investigators would claim that when people know they are being observed they behave and act differently and, as a result, covert observation is preferable. Also, in certain types of social science research, for example on the behaviour of inmates in prison, covert research may be the only way to gather meaningful data. Covert studies obviously raise a number of ethical issues. Ethics are discussed on pages 25–7.

Participant observation

Participant observation refers to a technique where the researcher becomes completely involved in the situation which is being researched. An example might be a theme park where on certain days a particular roller coaster ride is less popular, in spite of the fact that the same number of people are admitted to the park. Also the difference in popularity seems to correspond to days when there is a changeover of staff in charge of the ride. The researcher could join the workforce on the roller coaster and, hopefully, at first hand, be able to investigate the reasons for the change in popularity. This type of research emphasizes the interpretation of events and the interaction of the people involved. Work like this which looks at the behaviour of people is a very popular technique of ethnographic researchers.

There are, however, a number of general points to bear in mind if you are thinking about this type of data collection. First, you need to gain access and enter the research setting. If the research is covert then you become like an actor playing a part; you must not reveal your true identity. If you arouse suspicion as to your true identity, this could generate a hostile reaction and affect the overall validity of your work. If the research is open and the people around you know you are carrying out the work, then your inter-personal skills need to be excellent in order for you to gain their trust. Second, monitor your conduct during the research; be polite, respectful and interested in what is happening; you need to empathize.

How you record the data during participant observation can be difficult and this needs to be thought about before the research starts. Do you take notes, use a tape recorder, or use checklists? With the roller coaster example you would look for any activity which may affect people going on the ride. This could be a member of staff being rude to potential customers or some disagreement between staff which may cause fewer people on the ride, but how do you record it? Finally, when the data collection is over, you need to leave the research setting. This can be just as difficult as gaining access in the first place.

Non-participant (structured) observation

This is where the observer remains detached from the situation. You do not join in, but record what is happening. With the roller coaster example you may record the time it takes people to get on and off the ride. Perhaps one of the attendants on the low popularity days manages this in a slightly different way. Over the day the reason for the lower number of people on the ride becomes clear. The drop in the number of customers is not to do with the ride's popularity, but with the way it is managed by the two workforces on different days.

When carrying out this type of observation it is essential that you 'blend into the background' and don't let your presence get in the way. Try to position yourself in an out-of-the-way place and don't engage in long conversations with the people you are observing. Experience has shown that the longer you are in a setting the more your presence is accepted and the less obvious you become.

Ways of recording the observations

Two popular ways are the diary method and the use of checklists, as explained below.

THE DIARY METHOD

The keeping of a diary or log is an excellent way to record participant observation. Robson (1993) recommends that it may be written up in two sections. The first part, known as the *descriptive observation*, systematically reports on the events that take place, the characters involved, conversations that occur, together with a description of the setting, e.g., office, meeting room, etc. Don't forget to include the obvious, like time and date. These accounts should be completed as soon as possible while events are fresh in the memory. With overt research you may be able to make quick notes as you go along (field notes) and a small tape recorder used discreetly can prove very useful. With a covert study you have to rely on your memory.

The second stage is what Robson termed the *narrative account*. Here you reflect on the events and begin to identify ideas and trends arising from the descriptions. This early analysis and interpretation may alert you to particular issues which need to be observed again or which you have overlooked and which need to be included in following observations.

This reflective process is sometimes termed *analytical induction*. It is often difficult to stand back at this stage and be objective. One technique which, in the author's experience, helps is to imagine you are reading the diary of someone else, and study it as if you were carrying out research on that person. For example, suppose you were researching the ideas of a well-known management guru: reading their personal diary would give you an insight into how they developed their management ideas. It can also help if you write the description in the first person, but the narrative in the third person. It takes practice to keep a good diary, so some early attempts such as recording and reflecting one week in your life are good ways to begin. A diary can be a data collection method in its own right and this is explained on pages 38–9.

USING CHECKLISTS

With non-participant or structured observation you can use checklists, sometimes referred to as an *observation schedule*. You include in the schedule the type of features you want to record. These may include particular events, their frequency and duration. For instance, if you were observing a meeting you would have a seating plan, or when individuals spoke you would record the content and manner of their contribution. Was it friendly, challenging, did they agree or disagree with one another? You would also record the people who said nothing.

It is possible to buy ready-made schedules, but these tend to be expensive and may not suit your particular needs. If you decide to make your own, it is essential you choose the type of incident you need to record. An examination of the literature will help by alerting you to some of the key issues linked to the topic. It is important to be as focused as possible. You don't have the time to record everything, only be alert to what you need. A pilot study to iron out any problems and ambiguities is essential.

Advantages of observational research
These include the following:

- It is cheap, you can do it on your own, and it does not need expensive complex technology.
- It always works since you always observe something. Many people don't like to be interviewed and often throw postal questionnaires away.
- You experience a situation at first hand and this may give you a better insight when you interpret the data.
- Observation is a useful technique to research an organization of which you are a part, for example, when you are a placement student.

Disadvantages of observational research
These include the following:

- It is a time-consuming process and this needs to be borne in mind at the planning stage. Remember, dissertations have deadlines which must be met.
- With participant observation the researcher may become so involved in the situation that the research can take second place.
- You may witness and record situations which you do not agree with or hear conversations where you think one party is obviously to blame. Personal bias in these situations needs to be guarded against and overcome.

Indirect observation

In addition to formal observation techniques described, other information may be observed as a result of just being in an organization. This could include, for example, notices, minutes of meetings, letters and correspondence. You may also hear internal gossip about various parts of the organization. All this type of information from *indirect observation* provides a context in which you can set your research. Properly used, it can inform the research and certainly help when you come to interpret your results.

Diary methods

A useful data collection technique is the keeping of a research diary. You can either write one yourself or ask people involved in an investigation to keep one so they can note down their ideas, and reflect on personal circumstance and attitudes. Diaries are excellent when investigating the culture of an organization and changes within it, for example, at times of mergers and big re-structuring exercises. They are good to elicit opinion about different styles of management and leadership in an organization.

Diaries kept by other people ensure you collect information directly from respondents and several different writers' work can be compared on completion of the research. Also, the researcher has time to do other things. There are, however, disadvantages with asking people to keep diaries. They need to write reasonably well, and often require help at the start as to the sort of things they should record and how often they have to make an entry in their diary. They need constant encouragement that they are collecting information about the right things. Obviously anything they write is in confidence and this should be respected throughout the investigation. When asking other people to keep a diary, the following tips may help:

- At the start give a short informal presentation about yourself and the aims of the research.
- Provide a checklist of what you need in each diary entry: date, time, location, a description of events.
- Encourage volunteers to write the diary every day, while events are fresh in the memory. It is the content that is important – you are not in the business of correcting spelling and grammar.
- Encourage reflection about the issues being researched as well as a factual recall of a day's work. Some practice sessions here as a group will be beneficial and help build confidence. The techniques described for the observation diary (see pages 36–7) may assist. As with all aspects of data collection, this early preparation needs to be written up and included in the final dissertation. It corresponds to the pilot stage used in questionnaire design.

Case studies

As highlighted previously, a case study is not a single qualitative technique, since a number of methods is used. Many case studies include quantitative questionnaires, although they tend to make more use of descriptive evidence such as interviews and observation.

A case study may be defined as an extensive study of a single situation such as an individual, family or organization. Johnson (1994) defines a case study as 'An enquiry which uses multiple sources of evidence. It investigates a contemporary phenomenon within its real life context when the boundaries between phenomenon and context are not clearly evident.'

A well-known example is the study by Lane and Roberts (1971) on the strike at Pilkingtons in the UK. This study reported on various aspects of the strike. Interviews were held with senior management, strikers and shop stewards about their opinion of, and attitude towards, the strike. Information about the strike was collected from newspapers and by observing the strike committee in action. In fact, one of the authors spent the last three weeks of the strike observing the strike committee on a daily basis.

A dissertation example would be to study the introduction of a new computer system to a company. The research would look at the company before and after the introduction. The benefits and limitations of the system would be assessed. The effects on the workforce, management and clients could also be considered. A case study is, in reality, a detailed example investigated from all sides. Case studies are very popular and are especially good in situations which are complex and involve a number of different issues. They can be used in all aspects of management.

Types of case study

All case studies are inductive in that they report on the particular and specific, and then try to relate that to the general picture. They can be used either to generate theory and ideas about a topic, or to test out a theory to see if it occurs and applies in a real life situation.

There are different forms of case study. They may be described as follows:

- *Typical.* Here the organization studied is as typical as possible, for example, a large supermarket or general manufacturing company. The IT example above would fall into this category. A great many companies over recent years have taken on and introduced new technology and there is a lot of literature on the subject. This type of research is often used to test and examine accepted ideas about a subject.

- *Atypical.* Here the example is unusual and out of the ordinary. It is a 'one off'. The Pilkingtons strike was such a situation; it does not happen every day. Case studies like this add to knowledge and may initiate in the development of new theories and ideas about a subject.

- *Precursor studies.* With large research projects case studies are sometimes used at the start and act as precursors to identify the issues involved before the research is planned in detail.

- *Multiple case studies.* If time is available it is a good idea to study two or more similar examples. This allows for a comparative treatment and, as a result, helps build and confirm accepted theory.

The main question you need to answer is why you have chosen a case study approach in the first place. This may come down to cost, time or accessibility (especially if you are on placement). These are valid reasons and need documenting in the final write up.

The importance of context and background

As a case study tends to look at one example, it is essential that its context and background are described and explained in order to provide a full picture of the situation under investigation. With the strike example it would be necessary to provide some account of the factors which led up to it. A description of the company would be necessary to appreciate how the roles and duties of management, workforce, and other groups all relate to one another. With case study research, because of its uniqueness, it is important to 'set the scene' for the reader. This gives the research more credibility and makes it academically more valid.

The contextual features to note with a case study could include:

- the history and location of the organization: how it has developed over time to its current position;
- details of any similar case study research to help in the comparison of ideas and theory;
- an account of the national and possibly international picture. If you were working with a small building firm, some working knowledge of how the British building industry is organized may provide relevant background material;
- the current management structure of the organization being studied and how it works on a 'day-to-day' basis;
- the role and influence of government and other institutions (both local and central). Changes in law, tax rules, etc. all affect business and these may have a bearing on the case in question;
- the role of currently accepted theory. If you were looking at motivation in a company you would need to review the theories of motivation against what was actually happening in the company.

An important feature to watch out for when describing the context and background of a case study is that you do not take it too far. For instance, if you were investigating the marketing strategy of a company you would obviously need to look at the suppliers of raw materials and the client base, but it is not essential, and indeed it is unwise, to go into unnecessary detail.

Techniques used in case studies and the value of triangulation

A characteristic feature of case studies is that they employ a variety of different techniques. These include questionnaires, interviews, observation and diaries. All the advice about their planning, piloting, and execution needs to be followed. Using a number of methods allows you to triangulate the research (see pages 66–7) and this makes it more robust and valid. You can also use the various techniques at different stages. You may start with a questionnaire, which identifies certain interesting features which can be examined in more detail at later interviews. Questionnaires, for example, may ask people about their daily working practices and these can then be looked at by using observation techniques.

Advantages of a case study approach

The case study is an excellent vehicle for a dissertation. It is an approach that is especially suited to small-scale research and may well appeal to a placement student out in industry. Some advantages are the following:

- It can be carried out by the single researcher.
- It is relatively cheap and not dependent on expensive technology.
- A case study will always generate empirical data and information; you will not be solely dependent on already published work. The data may not be present in vast amounts, but it will always be interesting and specific to the example under scrutiny.
- It takes place in a natural setting within an actual organization. This gives the work a 'reality' which is often absent from surveys and similar types of investigation. A case study looks at the whole situation and the researcher (you) sees the inter-relations as they happen. This background is useful when you come to write up the work.

Disadvantages of a case study approach

With a case study approach there are a number of limitations as follows:

- With a single atypical case study it is often difficult to separate out what is unique to the organization involved and what is common to similar organizations.
- The whole issue of generalization needs to be handled with caution. The degree to which you can relate to the general position is often limited. At the writing up stage this caution needs to be stated quite clearly. It is essential that the generalizations arise from the research carried out, rather than what you think might be the case. Case study research tends to be subjective, but it is a good idea to keep the word 'objective' in mind when writing up.
- Case studies can generate a lot of information, since each different method used produces its own findings. The analysis and interpretation need to be handled carefully and in a very logical, systematic way. Again, when done effectively, this strengthens the academic argument you are presenting.

Action research

In recent years action research has attracted a lot of interest. Most of what is written about it concerns education contexts, focusing particularly upon teachers and the teaching–learning process. Less has been written about action research and management, although Gill and Johnson (1991) do give a useful account.

Action research may be defined in a number of ways. For example:

The study of a social setting involving the participants themselves as researchers with a view to improve the quality of action within it. (Rapoport, 1970)

Action research is small-scale intervention in the functioning of the real world and a close examination of the effects of such intervention. (Halsey, 1972)

The study of a social situation with a view to improving the quality of action within it. (Elliott, 1980)

What is implicit in all three definitions is that the researcher is interventionist in the research. The research is linked to a plan of action to bring about a change, which in turn brings about an improvement. In other words, action research is about a professional (e.g. manager) studying their own practice in order to improve it. For this to work there needs to be constant reflection of the issues being considered and the results from this reflection are then fed back into the research. The whole process is cyclic, and this, together with the critical reflection, is needed to identify and implement any improvements and changes, all of which make it a very time-consuming process.

Action research is like case study work in that one situation is studied by using a number of different data collection methods. It is, however, different in that the concept of improvement is always present and mandatory.

Action research because of its complexity is mostly used by masters and PhD students. However, for certain students on placement, action research could, in the right circumstances, be an excellent research strategy to use. A common theme present in action research is the management of change over time and how it involves people. This means that issues of confidentiality, access and the difficulty of remaining detached are all present and need to be taken on board during the research.

A suggested method for carrying out action research

The whole process is cyclic and uses techniques such as interviews, focus groups, diaries and observation. It is concerned with planned and evaluated interventions which involve groups or individuals who want to improve their professional practice. A number of different models on how to conduct the research have been described along the following lines. The research normally takes place in 4–5 stages depending on the problem being investigated.

STAGE 1 – THE START

Here the issues involved are identified, and the problem for improvement is looked at from a variety of standpoints. This stage is all about gathering information. The literature is searched and as much information as possible about the situation in question is collected and sifted through.

STAGE 2 – PLAN OF ACTION

Using a number of appropriate data collection methods, more detail is gathered and evaluated. As a result, a plan of action to improve the problem is worked out.

STAGE 3 – ACT, OBSERVE AND MONITOR

The action plan is put into practice and all changes noted. Again a number of methods is used (e.g. interviews, observation) to collect evidence about the success or otherwise of the introduced plan.

STAGE 4 – REFLECT

The effects of the action plans are subjected to critical reflection. This forms the basis for further planning, action and review. The critical reflection needs to be carried out in a systematic way and one method is to ask a series of questions. The type of question will vary depending on the research, but could be along the following lines:

- What are the salient features of this issue or problem?
- Why is it an issue or problem in the first place?
- What outcome(s) would you regard as desirable?
- What actions do you think will deliver these outcomes?
- Why do you think these actions will achieve these outcomes?

STAGE 5 – REPEAT STAGES 2–4

Using the evidence and results from the reflection the action plan is changed and the whole process starts again in order to bring about continued improvement.

Finally, as with all academic research, the work is written up. Since this type of research is a very fluid and continuous process involving repeated cyclic action and critical reflections, it is difficult, and inappropriate, to write it up in the conventional dissertation layout (see pages 135–40). It is better to produce a historical account – a kind of story which describes and recounts how the research developed over time. Provided all the salient features of academic writing are present, the literature cited and other academic criteria satisfied, then all should be fine. It would be wise, at this point, to take the advice of your supervisor.

In summary, action research provides an opportunity to do something very different. Note, however, it should always result in action and research, even though the balance between the two can vary in different studies. Sometimes the research element is based on conveying the understandings of the whole picture to all the people involved in a situation. In this context the research outcomes would include an account of the processes carried out, the rationale for actions taken, the perceptions of those involved, the data on which the conclusions are drawn and, if appropriate, the relationship to the work of similar studies.

Like all approaches to research, action research has its limitations. It is not appropriate for making generalizations which might apply to the wider population as a whole, and there is a danger that the researcher becomes too involved in the whole process. Its strength, however, lies in the understanding it can provide to a particular case, and in helping to facilitate an improvement in that situation.

5 Techniques of quantitative research, including sampling and triangulation

Introduction

An overview of quantitative research was given in Chapter 3 (see page 24). Quantitative methods have their historical origins in science and the approach is sometimes referred to as the 'scientific method'. It is based on the collection of facts and observable phenomena, and scientists use these to deduce laws and establish relationships. Research in business and management also uses quantitative methods and these provide a more objective base to guide professional practice.

Quantitative research describes, explains and tests relationships. In particular, it examines cause-and-effect relationships. The diagnostic feature is that the techniques used always generate numerical data. The data collected is then analysed. The analysis can be simple in mathematical terms involving the production of tables, charts and diagrams (e.g. pie chart, bar chart, etc.). This type of interpretation is referred to as *descriptive statistics*. The analysis can be more complicated and involve complex mathematical procedures and statistical tests of significance. This is termed *inferential statistics*.

As previously discussed, you are not expected to use every technique available, only the ones most suitable to your dissertation topic. With quantitative research, especially if mathematical and statistical procedures are involved, you must feel confident in using them. If you need inferential statistics, and mathematics is not one of your strengths, you may be well advised to get extra help before you start. It is essential with any method that you fully understand all its implications. As highlighted earlier, a 'mix' of qualitative and quantitative techniques to triangulate a topic is a good thing. It provides a range of perspectives to interpret a topic.

A type of dissertation which could use quantitative techniques is one on marketing, where the effectiveness of different marketing strategies is compared. Another example could be a dissertation about the introduction of a new administration procedure into an organization; the effects before and after the introduction could be investigated. A quantitative approach is often used in studies where the financial positions of different companies are compared and where financial trends and implications are examined.

In business dissertations two main methods are used to collect numerical data. These are surveys and experiments. Before they are described, the general features of quantitative techniques are explained.

General points about quantitative data collection techniques

Quantitative research sets up a hypothesis or theory. This is a proposition which is tested and, depending on the results of the test, the hypothesis or theory is either accepted or rejected. This type of research is deductive in that from the general situation, inferences can be made about a specific example. In other words, you start with a theory which applies in every case and the data collected either supports or rejects the theory. Quantitative research is, therefore, often termed *hypothetico-deductive*.

The emphasis is on measurement and testing, and numbers are always involved. Numbers alone (e.g. 5, 15, 34, etc.) mean very little. They must have units of amount (e.g. metres), position (e.g. 3rd, 4th, etc.), or time (e.g. hours, seconds). It is essential at the planning stage to decide the form the results will take and how you intend to analyse them. Be clear in your own mind what has to be measured and observed. If any type of statistical analysis (e.g. chi-square) is used, then you must decide at the start which tests to use, since most tests will only work with certain types of data. The number of samples needed and the size of each sample can also influence the choice of test. All this needs to be incorporated into the overall research design. This will strengthen the design and in turn support the validity of any conclusions. Too many researchers only think about results and what to do with them when the research is up and running.

Quickly draw tables and make calculations, etc., as you go along. This will give some idea as to the general trend the results are taking, and may alert you to the need for extra results. Many computer programs (e.g. SPSS, Minitab) are now available which will draw out various figures and make calculations. Use them, they save a great deal of time.

Quantitative data is either *discrete* (e.g. the number of cars a factory produces in one day is a definite number, i.e. 1, 2 or 3, etc.; it cannot be

3.5), or *continuous* (the amount of flour milled in a factory can be of any weight).

It is important to decide which scale of measurement you are going to use to collect the data. As noted before, only certain statistical tests can be used with certain types of data. The scales of data are as follows:

- Data may be *nominal* or *categorical*, e.g. cars in a car park can be sorted according to make, respondents in a survey may be male or female. In a questionnaire nominal or categorical data could be collected by the following type of question:

> Are you male or female? Please ring the appropriate word.

- Data may be *ordinal*, which means the data is on a scale with both classification and rank. For example, a political party selects candidates and then conducts a popularity poll. The results of the poll are Mr Matthews 34%, Mr Holmes 45% and Mr Thompson 21%. When set in order Mr Holmes is first, Mr Matthews second and Mr Thompson third. The 1–3 scale is the ordinal scale. An ordinal scale implies order, so in a questionnaire an ordinal question might read:

> How well do you rate your line manager? Please circle the most appropriate number.
>
> | Very good | Good | Fair | Poor | Very poor |
> |:---------:|:----:|:----:|:----:|:---------:|
> | 1 | 2 | 3 | 4 | 5 |

Note: Nominal (categorical) and ordinal data can only be used with non-parametric statistical tests (see pages 126 and 128).

- *Interval* data is where a scale is used and there are equal differences between points on the scale, but there is no true zero. It is arbitrary. Examples of interval data are time and temperature. In a questionnaire an interval data question might read:

> How many years have you worked for this company? Please enter the number of years in the space provided.   ....

- *Ratio* data is similar to interval data in that there are equal differences between points on the scale, but there is a true zero.

Length is an example of ratio data. In a questionnaire a ratio scale question could read:

> How many metres of fabric has your factory produced today?
> Please enter the number of metres in the space provided. ....

Note: Interval and ratio data can only be used with parametric statistical tests (see pages 126 and 129).

It is very likely with quantitative research that some of your results will be stored in a computerized database. If you intend to keep information about the people interviewed on a database and it is possible, from the information stored, that individuals can be identified, then you must comply with the Data Protection Acts. Advice and information about this can be obtained from

The Office of the Data Protection Registrar
Wycliffe House
Water Lane
Wilmslow
Cheshire SK9 5AX
Tel. 01625 545700
e-mail data@wycliffe.demon.co.uk

Techniques of data collection

Surveys

A survey is a way of describing and explaining some aspect of a population. Surveys are used, for example, in market research, opinion surveys and attitude surveys. Surveys are carried out by either interviews or questionnaires, or both. It is usually impossible, because of time, cost, size, etc. to consult every member of the population (termed the *sampling frame*), and a sample is, therefore, chosen. In most cases, a sample must be typical of the population and unbiased. Statisticians have developed techniques like random sampling, systematic sampling and stratified sampling to reduce bias and help ensure reliability. Sampling is explained in more detail on pages 59–65.

Interviews

Although interviews are mainly used when taking a qualitative approach (see pages 29–33) it is possible to code numerically the findings from interviews, so they can be used in quantitative research.

Questionnaires

For our purposes a questionnaire is regarded as a series of questions, each one providing a number of alternative answers from which the respondents can choose. Questionnaires are widely used in business, and popular with dissertation students. Although it seems obvious that if you want to know something from someone, you ask them a question, in reality the procedures involved in designing, writing and administrating questionnaires are complex. As with all aspects of research, never underestimate the planning needed. Again, a thorough background knowledge via searching the literature is essential.

Questionnaires generate data in a very systematic and ordered fashion. The responses to the questions are quantified, categorized and subjected to statistical analysis. At the early planning stage decide which kind of analysis (either descriptive or inferential statistics) you intend to apply because this will determine the way the questionnaire is designed.

Irrespective of the format, there are general points about questionnaires and their construction that apply to all. They are as follows:

- The quality of a questionnaire ultimately depends on the quality of the questions. Good, easy to understand questions will engage the respondents and encourage accurate replies.
- Be clear in your own mind why you are using a questionnaire in the first place, and decide exactly what your research objectives are. What are your information needs from the questionnaire? List all the items about which information is required. You may decide that it is easier to collect the data from an already published source.
- Choose whether to use postal or self-administered questionnaires.
- Keep questions as simple as possible; each question should only deal with one issue.
- A good attractive layout will encourage a reply. The questionnaire should be as short as possible and not excessive in length.
- Ask straightforward and unambiguous questions first. Start with questions about age, education and occupation and then lead up to more sensitive issues.
- Use 'closed' questions like 'Do you smoke?' where the response is straightforward. The answer is either 'Yes' or 'No'. Closed questions are quick to answer and easy to code for later analysis.
- Use 'open' questions where you need opinions. For example, 'Have you any comments to make about the finance department of the organization?' With this type of question, although subsequent

coding is more complex, you can be alerted to important issues which could be followed up in a second questionnaire or interview. If you want to gauge a degree of opinion, then ranking questions using the Likert scale may be used. An example is the line manager question already given to illustrate the ordinal scale.

- Group questions into sub-headings; each sub-heading can contain questions about similar topics.
- Avoid vague questions like 'Are you satisfied with your job?' The word 'satisfy' can have a number of meanings. Also avoid using very specialized vocabulary, unless you are sure it will be understood by the respondents. The wording of questions is very important; you should never lead or patronize.
- Give examples of how a question should be answered with simple instructions on how to complete the questionnaire, e.g. inform respondents to tick boxes, or circle appropriate numbers etc. Don't be afraid to guide the respondent on how to answer the questions.
- Unless anonymity and confidentiality are required, request the respondent's name and address should you need to contact them, and ask if they would like to be involved later, for example in follow-up interviews.
- With all questionnaires it is essential that either a covering letter (for postal questionnaires) or supporting rationale (for other types of questionnaire) is included with the questionnaire. This should state quite clearly why the questionnaire is being conducted, and who is doing it. You could explain that you are a student in your final year of university and the questionnaire is forming part of your dissertation. You could give access and allow them to read the final dissertation. Finally, thank them for their help in completing the questionnaire and assure them their privacy will be maintained if this is requested.
- Practise how you intend to analyse any information from the questionnaires in terms of either descriptive or inferential statistics. It is important that the method of data analysis is decided right at the start. From experience, if this is not agreed, it can cause a lot of trouble at a later stage, and can even invalidate the information collected.
- With all questionnaires it is essential that a pilot is carried out with a small number of volunteers. A pilot questionnaire will identify the ambiguous questions, alert you to problems of analysis and generally make the final version more relevant. As with other

aspects of data collection, time spent running the pilot and amending the questionnaire is not wasted. It is all written up and forms part of the methodology section of the final dissertation. When running the pilot, if possible, use respondents similar to your intended sample. If this is not possible, then ask a few friends to work through the questionnaires for you. This is better than nothing!

Types of questionnaire

In the main there are two formats for questionnaires:

- *Postal questionnaires.* Questionnaires sent by mail and either returned by mail or collected individually. Questionnaires are now being sent using e-mail.

- *Self-administered questionnaires.* One type is where the questionnaire is filled in by the researcher asking a respondent a series of questions. This is in a sense a very structured interview and the advice given for this type of interview still applies (see page 32). Questionnaires like this can sometimes be completed using the telephone. Also there is the case where the interviewer leaves a questionnaire with a respondent and agrees to call back at a later date and time to collect it when completed.

POSTAL QUESTIONNAIRES

Postal questionnaires are very popular with business students and they can form the basis of a good dissertation. One of the major problems with a postal questionnaire is, however, the low response rate, and even with a well-planned questionnaire using follow-up request letters and telephone calls, the response rate can remain low. It is, therefore, essential that when planning a postal questionnaire you decide how to handle this potential low rate of return.

One successful way is to find out as much as you can about the sample of people to whom you are sending the postal questionnaire. Therefore, if responses are only returned from one section of the sample, this may alert you to inferences from parts of the sample who did not respond. For example, a number of years ago the author carried out an industrial survey on the manufacturing industries of Humberside and their knowledge of new technologies. In particular, their awareness of genetic engineering and biotechnology and their importance to the manufacturing industry was investigated. A postal questionnaire involving over 2,000 companies was carried out. Certain manufacturing industries, e.g. engineering, failed to respond, and in the main, replies were received from pharmaceutical and chemical industries. As a result, it was possible with follow-up interviews to concentrate on industries which failed to return the initial questionnaire.

Other issues which can be used to help secure a good response rate are:

- The appearance of the questionnaire – it must look attractive, have a spacious layout with plenty of room for questions and answers.
- The wording of the questions must be simple and clear. The contents must be arranged so respondents have an opportunity to express their own views, as well as answering set questions. Every so often, after a block of questions on one topic, a side heading 'Have you any other comments?' will help. Leave space for the respondent to add their own comments, to a maximum of three lines.
- Instructions on how to complete the questionnaire must be simple, clear and bold. It sometimes helps to have these separately printed on coloured paper.
- Timing is important. If you are sending your questionnaires to senior managers, remember they are busy people. Your questionnaire should take no longer than 5–10 minutes at the most to complete. This means no more than two or three pages, which in turn means you must think carefully about what you want each question to ask.
- Completing the questionnaire should be regarded by the respondent as a learning experience. Early questions should be simple with a high interest value. The questions in the middle should be more difficult and searching, and the last few questions should also have a high interest value to encourage a return of the completed questionnaire.
- Large market research companies conducting postal questionnaires often offer inducements, such as competitions for cars, etc., in order to ensure a response. Unless you are a millionaire student, this scenario would be unlikely. Perhaps a small inducement, such as a tea-bag attached to the questionnaire with an invitation to take a 5-minute tea break in order to complete the questionnaire, might serve just as well, if not better!
- Use first-class postage and enclose a first-class stamped addressed envelope to encourage a reply.
- If questionnaires are not returned, then a follow-up letter reminding respondents is a good idea. The letter could

re-emphasize the importance of the study, and enclose another stamped addressed envelope and a second copy of the questionnaire. Some researchers make this second copy shorter, selecting only the most essential questions to which they need an answer.

Advantages of postal questionnaires
Some advantages are as follows:

- They are cheap and do not incur expensive travel and accommodation expenses.
- They allow for a large sample spread over a wide area to be surveyed.
- They are a relatively quick way of receiving a response.
- They avoid interview bias. Personal questions are often more willingly answered as the respondent is not face-to-face with the interviewer.

Disadvantages of postal questionnaires
Some disadvantages are as follows:

- As questions cannot be complicated, and need to be simple and straightforward, there is not a richness of information that is sometimes collected with other methods.
- You may not receive a spontaneous answer as respondents may discuss the questions with others before completing the questionnaire. As all questions are seen before they are answered, the answers cannot always be treated as independent. For example, if the question 'Can you name any dog food on the market?', was asked and the next question was 'Do you feed your dog Pal?', respondents may not have thought of any dog food for the answer to question 1, but could include 'Pal' as the answer after reading question 2.
- You cannot be sure that the named respondent has completed the questionnaire. A busy executive may ask a personal assistant to complete it on their behalf.

SELF-ADMINISTERED AND TELEPHONE QUESTIONNAIRES
With self-administered and telephone questionnaires you are in direct contact with the respondents and the good practice advocated for interviews (see page 33) applies. If you are going to deliver the form

to respondents' homes you need to make arrangements for the collection of the completed forms.

Telephone questionnaires can be useful and you can have the questionnaire already programmed into a computer so you can input the responses direct which saves time at the data interpretation stage. Computer aided telephone interviewing (CATI) can speed up the whole process and, if it is available, should be used.

With self-administered and telephone questionnaires it is a good idea quickly to run through the completed questionnaire with the respondent to make sure all questions have been answered.

Experiments

An experimental study, often quoted in the literature, is that conducted by Mayo (1933). Mayo investigated how different working conditions, such as lighting, shorter working hours and varied rest breaks (in total ten changes were looked at) affected productivity. The experiments took place in Western Electric's Hawthorne Works in Chicago between 1927 and 1932. The research showed that productivity increased whether the lights were bright or dim, whether the working day was long or short, and so on. The only explanation, Mayo concluded, was that the employees felt part of a team and simply not parts of a machine. There had been communication between the workers and the researchers, and as a result the workers felt more valued and also more responsible both for individual and group performance. This self and group esteem was more influential on productivity than changes in the working environment. Obviously the results surprised the researchers who naturally expected that changes in working conditions would have a great effect on productivity. Mayo's work is often quoted, and now an unintended effect as a result of a research experiment caused by subjects knowing they are part of the experiment is often referred to as the *Hawthorne effect*.

As can be seen from Mayo's work, experiments are used where the researcher deliberately sets out to control and manipulate all aspects of the situation. There is always a high degree of control. Experiments investigate the relationship between cause and effect. They determine whether a change in one factor (the independent variable) causes and produces an effect in another factor (the dependent variable). The researcher sets up a situation where the independent variable (in some cases there may be more than one) is brought into play and the effect on the dependent variable is recorded as a result. There may be instances where there is more than one independent variable, in which case each one is tested in turn and the effects on the dependent variable noted.

In science the experimental approach is the classical method of research and because of the nature of the discipline, especially with the physical sciences, with laboratories and special equipment, it is possible to have strict controls and even replicate an experiment a number of times. Business and management are very different. Large organizations are constantly changing and many of the changes happen only once. Imagine a large company is introducing a staff appraisal policy. It would be possible to examine the before and after effects, but it would be impossible to repeat the whole introduction.

However, there are times in business research when an experimental approach can be used. Suppose you are investigating the links between employment and the acquisition of IT skills. Given that IT plays such a major role in business today, you could assume that a person is more likely to be unemployed if their IT skill base is low. An experimental prediction like this is called a hypothesis. The independent variable is the employment factor and the IT skills level the dependent variable. Two groups of people could be used: one in employment and the other out of work. The IT skill level of each group could be measured and the results collected. On closer inspection the situation is not so clear-cut. There are a number of features, all of which could influence the results. Would it matter if some of the employed were joiners, teachers, or lawyers, or would they need to be in the same job? How would you measure the level of IT skills? Would you expect simple keyboard skills or a deep understanding of programming? Would the age of the people matter and would you need to know the proportion of men to women in the experiment? Finally, how do you know if the results have arisen by chance or because the presence of IT skills can actually affect your chances of employment? Here you may need to use some form of statistical test of significance.

Given all the pitfalls, an experimental approach, if carefully applied, can be used with great effect with dissertations especially in marketing. Examples of titles include 'The sales effectiveness of a new display', 'The impact of retail price change on market share', 'The effect of a different package design on sales'. In much of business and management research the independent variable is often a categorical or classification variable. For instance, to determine the effect of a training programme on staff, the independent variable is the training programme and the effects it causes the dependent variable.

As with any form of research, if you are going to take an experimental approach, planning, literature searching and giving general thought to the whole process are essential. Experimental design, if correctly used, can produce work of a high quality and is suitable for a business dissertation.

Types of experimental design
In practice there are different ways of carrying out an experiment. The way chosen depends on the facilities available and local conditions.

THE ONE-SHOT CASE STUDY
Here the group is exposed to a treatment and this is followed by a measure. An example would be to allow a group of administrators to attend a one-day workshop on report writing skills. After the day they may be more effective at writing, hence it could be argued that this was the result of the workshop. However, the result could also be due to other things connected with home or other aspects of work, etc.

THE ONE-GROUP PRE-TEST POST-TEST DESIGN
Here the subject is pre-tested before the treatment and then tested following the treatment. If you want to see whether there is going to be a change, it is a good idea to gauge the situation before the change happens. In the case of the administrators, some assessment of their writing skills before the one-day workshop would obviously strengthen the results of any experimental treatment provided by the workshop.

THE STATIC GROUP COMPARISON
Using a pre-test can indicate if a change has occurred, but it does not necessarily indicate that the treatment is the reason for the change. In our example the administrators might have seen a programme on TV about effective writing and this could have influenced the results. This can be overcome by having two groups of administrators, and subjecting only one of them to the one-day skills writing workshop. In this situation it can be assumed that both groups have had the same outside influences, therefore, if the treatment group responds better it can be assumed that the one-day workshop is having some effect.

The idea of having two groups, one subjected to the treatment (i.e. the workshop) and one not subjected to the treatment illustrates a very important concept with experimental design. It is the use and need for controls. In a scientific laboratory, controls are easy to arrange, but in real life they are difficult. Some idea of comparison, however, incorporates the concept of a control and this helps strengthen an experimental type investigation. The argument is also strengthened if the two groups of administrators are as identical as possible, and chosen at random without bias. The importance of sampling is discussed on pages 59–60.

THE PRE-TEST POST-TEST CONTROL GROUP DESIGN
This form of design is particularly robust. Both groups are pre-tested at the start, one group receives the treatment, the control does not, and both groups are post-tested at the end.

Other types of experimental design

A number of more sophisticated designs are available. Some of them can be quite complex, and not always suited to the undergraduate dissertation. One form that may be useful is what is termed the *quasi-experimental approach* (quasi = as if).

It is very difficult in the world of business to replicate true experimental conditions. The researcher will not be able to manipulate all the variables, controls and other factors which should be present in a true experiment. It may be possible, however, in certain situations to make a good approximation. This is termed a quasi-experimental approach. The concept of control and experimental groups is present, but normally not chosen in a random fashion. A dissertation example where this form of investigation may be useful is if you want to research some change that has occurred in an organization, for example, the introduction of flexitime, a staff appraisal policy, or the changes in staff morale following a re-organization of senior management. With this type of investigation you do get a before and after effect. However, because the procedures are not as precise as with true experimental designs, any results may be subject to wide interpretation.

Procedure for carrying out an experiment

The following scheme has been adapted from Creswell (1994).

1. *Identify a problem that is agreeable to the experimental method.* If we look again at some of the examples identified earlier, it could be along the lines of the introduction of a management training programme for personal assistants to senior managers.

2. *Formulate the hypothesis and identify the variables.* With the given example, the hypothesis could read 'To ascertain whether the

introduction of a management training programme will influence the effectiveness of senior management personal assistants'. The independent variable is the management training programme, and the dependent variable will be what is going to be measured, i.e. the effectiveness with respect to the personal assistants.

3. *Choose the subjects to be tested.* Here we need to choose the personal assistants, and decide whether we choose all of them in an organization, or a sample.

4. *Selection of a suitable experimental design.* Let's assume we are dealing with a big company and there are lots of personal assistants and senior managers. In this case the pre-test post-test control group design is the most appropriate. You need to select the design which best suits the situation at hand.

5. *Carrying out the experiment and collecting the results.* This is perhaps the most challenging and interesting part, and as with all research you should allow the literature on the subject to inform your thinking. How are you going to test effectiveness in the pre-test and post-test situation? Do you intend to carry out some test on the personal assistants, or interview the senior management as to the effectiveness of their personal assistants? The ways you collect the data at this stage can be various, e.g. interviews, questionnaires, asking the personal assistants to keep diaries, and so on. Don't confuse the overall approach you are taking, which is an experimental one, with the way you are collecting the data to support your approach. As stated on page 20, methodology (approach) and data collection (methods) are not the same!

Sampling

With any form of research such as surveys, it is usually impossible to question every member of the population involved. For example, if your dissertation was about UK DIY retailing you should, in theory, question every DIY outlet in the UK (i.e. you would carry out a census). Obviously, this would be impossible to do in the time available, and you would have to confine your research to a limited number of outlets, i.e. you would use a sample. You would try to ensure, unless there was a valid reason otherwise, that your selected sample was truly representative of the population of DIY outlets. With any research the total population in question is termed the *sampling frame* and the individuals within the population are called *sampling units*. Examples of sampling frames are students in your university, all the DIY retail outlets in the UK, packets of a particular brand of chocolate produced in a factory and so on. The sampling units are, therefore, the individual students, outlets and the bars of chocolate.

Samples are useful in research. They save money and time; it is virtually impossible to investigate every sampling unit of the population. Also, because the number of units is limited, more time is available to collect more data than would be possible if a census was being conducted.

Compiling the sampling frame

When using samples the production of the sampling frame is the first step. Good starting points are directories, such as the Yellow Pages, if you want to identify local populations of shops, restaurants and similar services. Local authorities and trade associations sometimes produce lists of various types of company and organization. There are also professional mailing companies who will provide the sampling frame and lists of address labels to use in postal questionnaires etc., but these can prove expensive. It often better to compile your own sampling frame. As mentioned previously, the author carried out a survey of the manufacturing industries of the former county of Humberside. Searching the literature located a regional directory published by the Yorkshire and Humberside Development Association which listed all the manufacturing industries – this provided a basis for the sampling frame which was augmented from other published sources. Good library skills were, therefore, needed at this stage of the research.

An accurate sampling frame is very important as it helps to reduce bias, and ensures that the sample used truly represents the population from which it is taken.

Methods of sampling

There are two basic ways of choosing samples: random (probability) sampling and non-random (non-probability) sampling and they are outlined below. Some of the techniques (e.g. quota sampling) are not necessarily suited to a dissertation, but an appreciation of each may help you when making a final selection.

RANDOM (PROBABILITY) SAMPLING

This works best with a very accurate and up-to-date sampling frame and is the preferred method if you intend to carry out any form of statistical analysis. With random sampling every sampling unit or member of the population has an equal chance of being selected. Each member of the sampling frame is given a number starting at 0 and the sample is selected using either random number tables or numbers generated by a calculator or computer. It is essential to realize that it is only the method of sampling that is without bias; the final sample selected may very well be biased. For example, if you were investigating some financial aspect of the European agricultural policy you would hope that the sample would represent all countries of the EU, but with random sampling it is possible for the final sample to be drawn from the same country.

There are three techniques of random sampling:

1. *Simple random sampling.* The required sample is chosen from the sampling frame by selecting the numbers as previously described. This technique is good where the sampling frame is not too large and each unit is easily accessible. The only issue you need to decide is whether to sample 'with' or 'without' replacement. If the item with the same number can be used more than once it is termed sampling 'with' replacement. This means that the data from a particular unit can be used more than once. Sampling 'without' replacement is where each item may not be used more than once, and another number (or sampling unit) is selected. From a statistical point of view, sampling without replacement is more precise and is preferred. Occasionally you may select a number above the top number of the sampling frame, e.g. the sampling frame numbers 1–40 and you select 41. Simply disregard the number and carry on until you have the sample size you need.

2. *Systematic random sampling.* With large sampling frames simple random sampling can be difficult and awkward. A better way is to arrange the population in some sort of order, e.g. alphabetical, and then choose the nth member of the list after selecting the starting point. For example, if your population is of 100 units and you want a 20% sample, you would select every fifth item on the list once the starting point chosen by random number tables is selected. If the starting point was 2 the numbers selected from your list would be 2, 7, 12, 17, and so on until all the sample was chosen. Systematic sampling is relatively quick to use and is preferred where large-scale sampling is needed.

3. *Stratified random sampling.* Here the population is split into layers or strata, which in reality are very different from one another. Examples of strata include gender, age groups, occupations, and income levels. If it is to be used correctly, stratified random

sampling requires clear and distinct groups showing in what proportions they are present. For instance, if you were investigating the operation of flexitime and how it affects its male and female employees you would need to know the proportion of men to women in the company. Suppose the company employs 60% women and 40% men, the technique of sampling is as follows:

Decide on the sample size (say 300).

Divide the sample into two sub-samples with the same proportions as groups in the population (180 and 120).

Select at random from within each group (stratum) the appropriate sub-sample (180 women and 120 men).

Add the sub-sample results together to obtain the figures for the overall sample.

Stratified sampling lessens the occurrence of one-sidedness as can be present in simple random sampling. Provided the population can be split into quite separate and distinguishable strata, stratified sampling is a very precise technique to be used.

NON-RANDOM (NON-PROBABILITY) SAMPLING

There are often situations where it is impossible to determine accurately the sampling frame. Also because of the nature of the research and dissertation, you do not need to make detailed statistical analyses. In such instances you can use what are termed non-random sampling techniques. With some qualitative research you need to sample with a definite purpose, and the approach therefore is subjective. Moreover, because of the nature of the work, you may be required to look at particular samples, as with a case study, which exhibit the characteristics you want to explore.

There are three main ways to use non-random sampling: cluster sampling, quota sampling and purposive sampling.

1. *Cluster sampling.* Within a population there often exist natural subgroups which can be termed clusters. For instance, if you were looking at the training needs of business and management students, and the population consisted of all business and management students attending local education authority sixth form colleges in the UK, the colleges under one authority would

make a natural cluster. With cluster sampling a random sample of the clusters is chosen, and then sampling takes place within each chosen cluster. The advantage of this sort of sampling is that you do not need a complete and accurate sampling frame. You only need a complete list of the sampling units within your chosen cluster. Cluster analysis is non-random and it is different from stratified sampling in that the clusters are similar to one another, in this example, sixth form colleges.

2. *Quota sampling*. This technique is used a great deal with market research surveys, especially where street interviews are used. The population is divided into groups, e.g. gender, income level etc. A number of interviewers is employed and each interviewer is informed of the number of groups they have to sample and the number of people (i.e. the quota) in each group they have to interview. It is up to each interviewer to decide how to locate and organize their prescribed quotas. After the interviews all the data is collated together to form the complete sample.

    Quota sampling has a number of advantages. It is relatively quick to arrange, and there is no need for a sampling frame. From a theoretical perspective the main disadvantage is the presence of interviewer bias. There is no check on how respondents are chosen, for example, the interviewer may select only men or women, or senior citizens or anyone they think will stop and be interested in taking part. For the undergraduate dissertation quota sampling is not usually a good idea, since it works best with a large population and a number of trained interviewers being involved.

3. *Purposive sampling*. This is often called judgemental sampling, because the researcher picks the sample they think will deliver the best information in order to satisfy the research objectives in question. This method is particularly good if you are thinking of using a grounded theory approach (see page 110). Under this general heading of purposive sampling different types of sampling can be described. Where there is the need to focus on one particular and somewhat unusual issue, there is what is termed *extreme sampling*. If you need to identify a range of topics you would then need to search out samples that could provide a variety of information, and this is *heterogeneous sampling*. Alternatively, you may need to examine one issue in detail, and then search for samples that are more or less the same. This is

termed *homogeneous sampling*. Where there is the need to examine controversial and contentious issues you would select what is termed a *critical sample*. This type of sampling gives you enormous scope but, like all aspects of research, the rationale for a particular method needs to be well articulated and described.

Sample size

You may have decided that for your dissertation a systematic random sampling method is the best. You now have to decide on the sample size (the number of sampling units to take). Although this is a simple question, it is not a simple question to answer. Common sense would possibly suggest that a large sample is better than a small one, since an increase in sample size does decrease what statisticians call sampling error. However, there are instances when this is not the case. If the sampling frame consisted of very similar types of respondent, a large sample would not be needed. What is more important in this situation is the accuracy of the information collected from the sample. What guarantees accuracy is the careful design and execution of, for example, the interview schedule, and the design of the questionnaire, etc.

The sample size chosen is usually a compromise between the practical issues (e.g. time, money, etc.) and theoretical considerations involved. Statistical tables have been calculated which show the degree of precision (sampling error) which is theoretically obtainable for samples of different sizes. These are based on mathematical considerations which take into account accurate sampling frames, perfect sampling, compensation for the influence of bias, non-response etc. For very large samples you are recommended to consult specialist statistical textbooks (see Annotated Bibliography, Chapter 12). If you only have time to use small samples the following 'rule-of-thumb' normally will suffice:

1. If you are going to use any quantitative and statistical techniques decide at the start what type of data (e.g. nominal, ordinal, etc.) you are going to collect, and which test you are going to use. This in turn often dictates the sample size.

2. If the population is about 50 or less, sample the whole population if time allows. This means you carry out a census rather than a survey.

3. If you have to sample a population of 50 or more, then try for a sample of around 30 using an appropriate technique described. If

you have to have a sample of less than 30, statistical tests like the Student's t test may be used.

4. If your sample is being divided into categories, as for example with stratified sampling, aim to have at least five sampling units in each category. For instance, if you were going to carry out a survey gauging people's preference for fruit drinks, the following layout could be used:

Fruit Juice Preference	Male	Female
Orange	5	5
Grapefruit	5	5
Tomato	5	5
Pineapple	5	5

Each cell in the table has five people, and the total sample therefore equals 40. If you decide to sub-divide the male and female groups say into age categories, for example people above 30 and people below 30, this immediately doubles your sample size to 80. Although at first this might appear a simple thing to do, in practice you have doubled the amount of work. You now have to interview 80 people, as opposed to 40. This also causes an increase in travel, transcription of tapes, and so on. It is far better to keep the sample size small and manageable.

Sampling and Qualitative Research

There is no reason why the principles of sampling should not apply equally to qualitative research when selecting individuals for observation techniques or interviews. In fact, the use of non-probability sampling, especially purposive sampling, is ideal with case study and action research. Purposive sampling allows for variation and enables particular choices to be made relative to a particular research situation.

Bias

When selecting samples it is important to bear in mind the concept of bias. Harper (1991) defines bias as 'allowing a particular influence to have more importance than it really warrants'. The whole purpose of sampling is to gather information about the population. Unless a special sample is needed for a particular reason, e.g. purposive sampling, you want the sample to represent the whole population, and as far as possible to have no bias.

Bias can arise because of a number of reasons:

1. *Sampling frame bias.* A poor, out-of-date and inaccurate sampling frame leads to bias. For instance, if you use a telephone directory to construct a sampling frame, you omit potential respondents who do not have a telephone or are ex-directory. Using the electoral register may miss out people who for various reasons have not registered.

2. *Researcher bias.* You the researcher may unwittingly introduce bias. You may make your questions too narrow, and as a result respondents in an interview do not have the opportunity to express themselves fully. On the other hand, your questions may be too broad and the answers so general that the final interpretations become diffuse and unfocused. If, as a young student, you are questioning someone much older than yourself, this may cause bias. The interviewee may want you to succeed and do well in your dissertation, and give you the answers they think you want to hear. In all good faith they may not be completely honest with you. In market research interviews there is interviewer bias which has already been mentioned.

3. *Non-response bias.* Non-response, especially in postal questionnaires, is always a problem and can generate considerable bias. You have no way of knowing how respondents would have answered the questions. People do not respond for a variety of reasons. Your questionnaire might look unattractive; they may have moved address, so they never received the questionnaire.

In reality, it is impossible to remove bias completely from any form of survey research. Sampling frames and respondents' opinions can change overnight. What is essential is that you recognize at the start the existence and the importance of bias and the potential influence it may have on your particular sampling and research methods.

Triangulation

So far, the techniques of quantitative research have been kept separate from those of qualitative research. Mention has been made, however, (see page 25) of the idea of combining methods together in the sense that the same dissertation topic may be studied via a variety of approaches. It could be argued that researching the same topic using a number of different techniques is complementary, with the outcome resulting in a more thorough understanding of the problem under investigation. The idea of combination is termed *triangulation*. The word originally comes from navigational practice where a number of reference points can be used to locate an exact position.

In research methodologies triangulation is a general term, and different authors on management research give it slightly different meanings. If, for example, the same problem is studied using both qualitative and quantitative methods this is referred to as *method triangulation*. For example, with case study research, questionnaires, diaries and interviews can all be used. Comparison of the results gives far more information about the topic under investigation. If results from the different methods point to the same inferences, this in turn strengthens the overall argument. This type of triangulation is good to use with a student dissertation. It provides you with an opportunity to use a number of different techniques. However, before you decide on the range to use, look at the strengths and weaknesses of each one as related to your dissertation topic.

If the same method of data collection is from different sources, and over different time-scales, this is often termed *data triangulation*. An example would be to follow the career paths of several managers over a number of years. As their careers developed you could question them (e.g. by interview) about how they saw their different positions, and how they achieved them. Obviously, this type of data collection is not normally suited to an undergraduate dissertation which has to be completed within one academic year.

Finally, there is what is termed *theoretical triangulation*. Here the theory of one academic discipline is applied to a research situation within another discipline. With business and management this is very difficult to achieve. By their nature they are wide in scope, and already have their roots in separate disciplines like sociology, psychology and economics.

In summary, for the majority of undergraduate business dissertations the use of a variety of data collection techniques should be encouraged, and method triangulation is perhaps the best one to use. It is essential, however, that the techniques are chosen with care and are relevant to the topic under investigation. Don't simply choose questionnaires and interviews because you like doing them and find them relatively straightforward. The final selection of techniques must relate to your overall research design, which in turn must be relevant to the aims of the research itself.

6   Writing a proposal

Introduction

Before beginning a dissertation most university students are required to submit an account which outlines the nature of their chosen subject. This is usually termed a proposal and you may be required, either to complete a special form, known as a proposal form, or to write an outline of what you want to do, using a prescribed format or guideline. This chapter reviews the various aspects of preparing an acceptable proposal; it looks at what a proposal is, why it is important, the various layouts which may be used, and the characteristic features found in a good proposal. Finally, you will find two examples of proposals, one acceptable and one unacceptable, with comments.

Although the things you write down at the proposal stage are not fixed in 'letters of stone', they should reflect that you have given some serious thought to the chosen subject, and made a real attempt to show how you intend to study it. A number of students, however, consider proposals a tedious and unnecessary chore. This is not the case. A good proposal indicates thorough preparation at an early stage and, in the author's experience, saves a great deal of time later on and always pays dividends. Good proposals mostly lead to good dissertations.

Note that this chapter does not consider the administrative details involved, for example, the dates for handing in proposals and the procedures they have to go through to determine whether they are approved or not. Course leaders and dissertation tutors are well aware of your concerns, and give students plenty of notice. Details of the administrative arrangements about dissertations are usually available on course noticeboards, in course handbooks, and the like.

What is a proposal?

A proposal is a summary of the work you have to do for the dissertation. It outlines the aims, methods and other features of the work.

It includes a statement as to the nature and purpose of the study, together with some account of the background of the subject. In short, it summarizes exactly what you want to do in the time available. Ways of presenting proposals vary from university to university, and the examples given below cover most of the information required in a thorough proposal. The required length of a proposal varies. Some institutions require up to eight or nine pages, while others require no more than two. In general, the average proposal is between four and six pages in length.

Why proposals are important and needed

In my experience many students can become intimidated at the prospect of producing a dissertation. A proposal starts the process off and makes you think carefully about what you want to do. It is a very important stage in the whole dissertation process and ensures that you have thought about all the issues involved. Working through a proposal makes you think about many things at once and helps organize your thoughts in a logical manner. It gives you confidence to progress with the work.

In the world of commercial research detailed proposals are regarded as essential. For instance, national funding bodies will not sponsor any form of research until they have received and approved a detailed outline of what the research entails.

From a university's point of view dissertation proposals are also essential. Most universities provide dissertation supervisors who guide and advise you. A good proposal ensures that you are allocated to a member of staff who has an interest and expertise in your chosen area. You may need to see your supervisor at an early stage in the drafting of the proposal. Be prepared for searching questions as to the feasibility and nature of your dissertation. As a result, you may be asked to revise your thoughts. All of this is designed to ensure that the final dissertation is a success. Remember, academic criticism is not a personal attack on you; it is meant to assist in refining the proposal in order to achieve a successful outcome.

Suggested proposal layouts

The following examples of proposal layouts include only the headings and any accompanying notes. They have been collected and adapted from a number of universities. Although some expect more detail than others, all require the student to give serious consideration to their chosen subject. Some universities provide special forms, while others give a series of headings and a suggested layout. With any proposal never forget to include your name and course details, and the majority also require you to sign and date the proposal. Finally, don't forget to keep a copy of the proposal for yourself.

EXAMPLE 1

Name:

Course Details:

Proposed Title:

Proposed Aims and Hypothesis:

Methodology: (Describe here how you propose to test your hypothesis; original primary research and use of secondary resources. When do you propose to undertake the research; does it involve work carried out in your placement year?)

Literature sources: (It would be helpful at this stage to review briefly any information you have read about your chosen topic. List the information sources you have identified to date.)

Reasons for choice of topic: (It would help if you outlined the reasons for your choice. Does it arise out of your placement year, general interest, seems like a good idea?, etc.)

EXAMPLE 2

Name and course:

Title of proposed dissertation:

Outline briefly the topic area including important debates and concepts.

What form will the research take? Is it pure research, applied research or action research?

Briefly explore the nature of the way you are approaching the problem. Are you taking a qualitative or quantitative approach and how is this influencing your choice of techniques?

List with reasons the techniques you intend to use.

Are there any potential political and ethical issues involved?

List your working bibliography.

| EXAMPLE 3 | Give a statement of the precise area/subject that you will cover and provide a provisional title. |

Aims and purpose of study:

Outline the research methods to be used and a justification for your choice.

Provide a preliminary outline of the information sources you have already identified. Briefly review them.

How does your dissertation arise out of the work already covered on your course?

What is the relationship of your dissertation to other subjects being studied in your final year?

Your completed proposal should be no more than 2 sides in length.

| EXAMPLE 4 | Name:
Course: |

Personal tutor:

Brief outline of research programme: (Include your aims, reasons for the choice and some outline of the work already carried out in the area.)

Details of interviews and other research methods you intend to use: (Include a rationale for your choice and why you have selected the identified methods.)

This is a particularly brief layout, but an account of the aims, some background literature and the selected research methods are still required.

EXAMPLE 5

Name:

Course:

The topic area: (Please give a brief discussion of the area chosen, the reasons for choosing it, its relationship to your degree and to the courses you have studied so far on your programme.)

Aims: (Please give a clear, precise statement of the problems to be analysed in the form of a hypothesis to be tested. The aims should, therefore, state the main purpose of the research.)

Literature review: (Please give a brief review of the literature sources you have consulted so far which have a bearing on your chosen topic area and aims. List full bibliographic details of the works you have consulted.)

Methodology: (Give brief outline of your methodology and how you intend to test your hypothesis. Give information about the type of data you expect to collect and the proposed form of analysis you will use after collection.)

EXAMPLE 6

Name of student:

Course:

Working title of dissertation.:

Aims of the dissertation:

Relationship to previous work:

Proposed methodology and research techniques:

Proposed plan of work and research timetable:

Resources required: (Do you need to borrow a tape recorder, camcorder etc.; do you need access to any particular computer software, e.g. NUDIST, to analyse your results?)

Form of presentation: (It is expected that most students will produce the traditional report format dissertation. However, some students may wish to include a video, etc. as part of their final submission. Please note this now. If at a later stage you wish to change the form of your presentation, this is normally acceptable provided you inform your dissertation supervisor in plenty of time.)

Bibliography: (List in an accepted academic style, e.g. Harvard system, any references identified in your proposal.)

Characteristics of a good proposal

The six examples above illustrate a range of proposal layouts currently used on a number of business and management programmes. Let's revise the key points identified using Example 6 as this one covers all the main points. It is important to restate that a proposal is not aimed at limiting your ideas and imagination; these are essential in any academic work. It is a way of getting you to think in practical terms about how you intend to research and write your dissertation.

The key areas to include in any proposal are:

- *Name and course.* Although it seems obvious to state your name and course, students often in haste forget to include them. Certain universities also ask students to add their enrolment or registration number.

- *Title.* Dissertations must have a title. At this early stage a holding or provisional working title will usually suffice. You can decide on the exact wording when the dissertation is nearly complete. However, even at the start aim for a title which gets over the idea of an investigation. A title which begins 'A study in ...' is normally too vague; decide whether you want to compare, collate, assess, etc. Don't worry if you end up with a long title. You are working on an academic document – you are not writing a catchy headline for a tabloid newspaper.

- *Aims.* Your earlier brainstorming plan (see pages 15–16) will help here. You must identify the questions your research is intended to answer. This is where careful planning pays off. Once the work begins you may find that aims change in emphasis and in number. This can happen with any research, but what is essential is that at the start you specify, as far as possible, the precise focus of the research, with the key concepts identified. When working on the aims attempt to give your work some originality by isolating how your research questions are different from what you already know about the subject. Ask yourself, from what you have read so far, how your overall approach is unlike that of other researchers.

- *Relationship to previous work – reviewing the literature.* At the proposal stage some attempt must be made to review the literature. Obviously, early on you cannot have read everything on the subject, but you should be able to list and summarize a working bibliography. A good start is to locate and read about ten recent articles which cover the main issues of the topic. An early visit to the library will also inform you as to the amount of literature on your subject. It is important to know what other people have written about your topic in terms of theory, current issues and professional practice. A thorough initial literature search may also help in deciding the best methodology and techniques to use. Keep details of all sources used and if they need to be written into your proposal use an accepted style (e.g. the Harvard system). The use of literature is so important that there is a separate chapter about it (Chapter 7).

- *Methodology.* This section of any proposal is vitally important; time spent working out the way in which data and information is to be collected and analysed is never wasted. Be prepared to spend some time on this section. How you study a problem is as important as the results you collect. A balanced methodological approach using appropriate well thought-out data collection techniques ensures the conclusions and recommendations you make at the end are more valid and credible. Results quickly gathered with no thought given to the methodological issues involved makes research meaningless. If you have little knowledge and experience of the practical issues involved with research it will help you to re-read the previous chapters.

 The key issues to address in the methodology section are:

- What is the overall methodological approach? Is it qualitative or quantitative? Are you going to take a special approach, such as action research, or use case studies?
- How does the approach fit in with the overall research design and what specific methods of data collection are you going to use, e.g. surveys, interviews, questionnaires, observation, etc.?
- If you propose to conduct interviews and questionnaires, how do you intend to use and select the sample?
- Is it possible to study the same problem using a combination of different approaches and techniques? Triangulation is very useful and is described on pages 66–7.
- How do you intend to analyse and interpret your results? Will there be any statistical analysis involved?
- Can you at this early stage envisage any practical limitations which could affect your data collection? Don't forget the basics like time and money. Your dissertation has to fit in with all the other work of your final year.

All this may sound daunting and off-putting; it's not meant to be. Once research starts, it is a very 'hands on' process and planning ahead keeps it in balance and perspective.

- *Plan of work – time-scale.* Not every proposal asks for this, but it may help if you can estimate how long each stage will take. Effective time management is essential. Dissertations have a deadline – a date by which they must be handed in. You need, therefore, to work backwards and estimate how long each stage will take. Don't be over-ambitious. All stages seem to take longer than originally planned, so allow for this in your early planning. Some students draw out elaborate charts to help them balance the time; anything that helps you is worthwhile. The ideal scenario may be to have all the early planning and literature search completed in the long vacation before your dissertation year. Collect all the data by the Christmas vacation and allow the time between Christmas and Easter for writing up. In the author's experience most dissertations are usually submitted in April or May.

- *Resources required.* As identified in Example 6, some universities require you to list any special equipment you need. Even if this is not required, some thought given to what you may need will certainly help at the planning stage. If you intend to use any computer software, be sure you know how to use it. Most dissertations have to be word-processed or typed. If you are not going to do it yourself, it is a good idea to make an early arrangement with someone who can help. If you intend to use a university machine, note that a lot of other students will be needing the use of a computer at the same time!

- *Form of presentation.* Again this was highlighted in Example 6. The general advice is that if you intend to vary from the traditional bound report format (e.g. an action research dissertation), talk it through with your dissertation or personal tutor. Universities often have regulations governing the ways in which dissertations and theses are presented, and you must adhere to them.

- *Bibliography.* As identified earlier if you have to list the books and articles you have read do so in an accepted university style. Advice on this is given on pages 142–5.

A final note. If you read through the given proposal examples you will see variations in layout and the information needed. Some require comment on political and ethical issues, links with work carried out in other parts of the degree course, or reasons for the choice of topic. However, the overall aim of any proposal is similar in that you have to give serious thought about all the processes involved.

Examples of completed proposals

Two examples are given, one acceptable, one unacceptable. Both are fictitious, but they have been based on the type of proposals prepared by a third year cohort on a BA (Honours) Business Studies degree. With each example, the fictional student's work is in normal print and the author's comments are given in italics.

EXAMPLE 1 – This proposal is very brief and not acceptable

Title of dissertation

How 'Green' is Business Studies?

The title is too vague; as it stands it means very little. You have no idea what the dissertation is going to be about, apart from that it is something to do with business studies and the colour 'green'. If the student intends that green should convey the idea of environmental issues, then this needs to be stated in the title.

Aims of the dissertation

To look at the various subjects taught under the umbrella of business studies, and re-assess them using a 'green' perspective, particularly within the subjects of economics and marketing.

The aim is too loose and ambiguous. How do the subjects quoted (economics and marketing) fit in with business studies? What is meant by a 'green' perspective?

Relationship to previous work

Broad ideas from economists like Schumacher, Galbraith, etc., from marketeers like Kotler and Saunders, and writers like Porter point to the concept of 'net national product' as investigated by the World's Bank Environment Department.

Apart from mentioning some well-known writers, little is given about the relationship between 'green' issues and the aims of the dissertation which wants to look at 'subjects taught under the umbrella of business studies'. From what is written it would appear that the student has read very little, and hopes to succeed by quoting a few well-known names. On a technical point none of the writers have been cited in a correct academic format; publication dates are not given.

Methodology

A comparison of government and world statistics. A study of the role of marketing and how it can be 'green'. Examples of successful companies will be used as a case study.

Like the previous sections, this section is equally vague. What techniques will be used to carry out the comparison? How will marketing and its 'greenness' be studied? Which successful companies will be used, and what does the student mean by the term 'case study'?

Plan of work

By December, all research work to be completed, and writing up to be finished by Easter.

Again, this is too vague. Taking the proposal as a whole you have no idea how the work will fit in to any proposed time-scale.

Resources required

Government statistics, economic forecasts and predictions, World Bank accounts.

All these are valid sources, but publication details and how the student intends to access them are needed.

Bibliography

Schumacher – all works.

Galbraith – all works.

Porter – all works.

This section also lacks details; specific publication details are required.

Overall comments on Example 1

This is obviously a poor dissertation proposal. It appears rushed and ill-conceived, and the student has given it very little thought. It would need to be re-submitted.

EXAMPLE 2 – This proposal is acceptable

Title of dissertation

An investigation into the strategic issues adopted by certain major business corporations in order to establish permanent internal consulting services.

Immediately you know what the dissertation is all about, i.e. strategy, big business, the establishment of permanent internal consulting services. In short, the title speaks for itself.

Aims of the dissertation

An internal consulting unit within a major business corporation is one which is permanently established to provide professional consulting services to other units within the same corporation. In recent years there has been an increase in the establishment of internal consulting units. Possibly promoted by recent global business trends, more and more large business corporations are providing their own consultancy services. It is the intention of this dissertation to examine different companies' approaches to the implementation of an internal consulting group. Specifically, the dissertation intends to answer the following questions:

- Why do major groups establish internal consulting units?

- How are they implemented?

- What demand is there for the consultancy services once the units are established?

- What are the missions, objectives and benefits from the units?

- What factors govern their success or otherwise?

- How do the big companies evaluate the experiences gained from the establishment of such units?

By answering the above questions, the dissertation hopes to bring available theory and practice together and add to the growing literature in the field.

Immediately, you feel the student has a good idea about the nature of the topic, and has formulated some precise research questions to investigate it. What is missing, however, is the role and nature of big business corporations which are referred to in the aims, and also in the title.

Relationship to previous work

One of the first publications dealing with internal consulting was by Dekom (1969) where internal management consulting was described as a new management phenomenon. Over the years a number of publications (e.g. Gale, 1970; Hoenke, 1970; Bellman, 1972; Allanson, 1985; Kubr, 1996) have developed the understanding of internal consulting. It has now become a professional, highly qualified and independent service, rather than part of a simple management service. Recent publications focus on the functional, conceptual and organizational issues of internal consulting. This dissertation will review the literature and the application of internal consulting with big business.

The student has identified a number of recent references, and would appear to have some knowledge of internal consulting. Again what is missing from this section is any mention of big business and how it relates to internal consulting.

Methodology

Both desk research and field research will be carried out. Desk research will focus on examining the literature. Field research will use a case study approach by identifying two or three big businesses where the role of internal consulting will be examined. At this stage the number of companies has not been identified, but it is hoped in the time available to consider at least two. Each company will be researched by carrying out interviews with selected staff, and by examining internal documents (e.g. minutes, internal reports, etc.) which are available. During my placement year I worked for a large pharmaceutical company and I have written permission from the company that I can use them in my dissertation. I intend to use semi-structured interviews as far as possible.

The student has chosen a case study approach and has identified a company which will serve as an example in the case study. Although the student has a good idea of the type of techniques they want to use, more detail could be given with respect to the selection of interviewees and the interview schedule to be used. However, overall the student knows how the data will be collected. What could have been included in this section is some account of how the data will be interpreted and analysed.

Plan of work

July 1997	Early proposal. Research into the literature.
August – September 1997	Detailed literature search. Proposal finalized.
October – December 1997	Visit to companies. Interviews carried out. Literature search continued. Preliminary data evaluated.
January 1998	Layout of dissertation decided. Gaps in literature and data identified.
February 1998	Literature search and data collection completed.
March – April 1998	Data evaluated. First draft of dissertation completed.
May 1998	Final draft agreed with supervisor. Final draft submitted.

This is a good plan of work, and thought has been given to the various stages involved.

Resources required

The main resources required will be:

- different literature, including magazines, newspapers, reports, etc.;
- internal papers of the examined companies;
- interviews, discussions and other conversations;
- phone, fax, e-mail;
- appropriate IT facilities.

Although the student could have given titles as to the different literature sources, in the main this is a complete list of items required to complete the dissertation.

Bibliography

To save space this has not been included, but the student quoted over 20 references, each one set out according to the Harvard system. The student also divided the list into those references cited in the proposal and those which provided general background reading and informed the train of thought in the production of the dissertation.

Overall comments on Example 2
Compared with the first example, this proposal is a lot more detailed, and the student has spent far more time in putting it together. What is absent is any real mention of the companies which will be used in the case study. Also more detail could have been provided with respect to the methodology. However, this student would have been allowed to continue with the dissertation on the condition that these deficiencies were addressed, and these would be monitored by the dissertation supervisor.

A final note

Proposals are an important stage in the production of a dissertation. As has been stressed throughout this chapter, early preparation pays dividends in the long term. Take time and effort at the proposal stage – it's well worth it.

7 Using the literature

Introduction

Throughout this book constant reference has been made to the importance of literature and how this can help set your dissertation in the context of what other people have done. This means you must access and evaluate as much of the published information as possible. In order to do this you need to have a good working knowledge of business and management information, the ways in which it is organized and classified, and the most effective way to retrieve and evaluate it. Nowadays information is available in many different formats such as books, periodicals, audio and video tapes, CD-ROMs and the Internet. The amount is increasing all the time. Given the relatively short time you have to complete a dissertation, you will not be able to read every single piece of published material, but with care, patience and good library skills you will be able to access a great deal.

This chapter is, therefore, about business and management information and the following topics are covered:

- Why you need information in the first place.
- The types of business and management information that are available. This includes primary book sources, secondary book sources, non-book sources, and electronic information sources.
- The organization of business and management information in libraries. In order to search effectively you need to know how libraries organize and classify their stock.
- Guidelines on making a literature search.
- The importance of evaluating the information. The material you collect for your dissertation is only part of the process. How you evaluate and use it is just as important, and this stage is often overlooked.

Why you need information in the first place

It is essential with any dissertation that you identify where the work fits in with previously published work. A knowledge of what's gone before will give you a 'state-of-the-art' background. This will help you to discuss the dissertation in its relevant context, together with any theoretical frameworks which may be involved. It may also trigger your imagination and help you set the work in a new and different light.

In summary, you need information to:

- ensure that your dissertation is not an unnecessary replication of work already carried out. It is perfectly acceptable to repeat research, but there needs to be a good reason for it. For example, do you doubt the methodology, disagree with the results, or question the theoretical underpinning of the research?
- inform your research design and methodological approach. This may provide a foundation for your chosen data collection techniques.
- provide the appropriate contextual, theoretical and background information.
- identify other researchers interested in the same subject area.
- identify gaps in the knowledge about your topic. You can then speculate why there are gaps. Is it because no-one has identified them before, or are the gaps, for whatever reason, somewhat difficult to research and study?
- confirm basic ideas and knowledge about the subject while identifying redundant and out-of-date concepts.
- identify contemporary and current thinking about the subject. You can then compare your work. A well-argued comparison is a very effective section to include in any dissertation. Search out secondary evidence from previous published work which can confirm and support your thoughts and ideas.
- Confirm your commitment and interest in the subject.

Never under-estimate the value of published work. It will form the basis of the literature review section of the final dissertation (see page 138). In the early stages of research a trawl through the literature can be a daunting exercise. What you need to do is constantly revise the information you collect and see its relevance in the wider context. The key to successful literature searching is to re-evaluate and assess the material as you go along. Points to think about at the evaluation stage are discussed at the end of this chapter.

Types of business and management information

This section lists information sources which will be useful in preparing a dissertation. There is a tremendous variety of information available. It includes books, articles, letters, committee minutes, diaries, company reports, audio tapes, video tapes, periodicals, and so on. Nowadays, information is also available on the Internet and in other electronic formats, e.g. CD-ROMs.

Information is classified into *primary material* and *secondary material*. Information which is new and original at its date of publication is termed primary material. It is up-to-date, detailed and accurate, and tends to be very specialized. Consequently, fewer people want to use it; it is expensive and sometimes difficult to trace. Secondary material contains information which has been published before. An example of a secondary source is a textbook. The author has used a number of different sources in preparing this book, and although it may have a different slant, most of the material it contains will be in print somewhere else. Secondary material is, therefore, less specialized and not so up-to-date. As more people want to use it, it is usually less expensive and easier to get hold of.

In preparing your dissertation you will need to use both primary and secondary material. The primary sources will provide details of previous research, while the secondary material tends to provide general background and theory. All the references and information sources listed in this section are available in large academic and public libraries. A useful exercise would be to find out what is available in your university.

A very useful general guide to introduce you to searching out business information is:

Spencer, N. (1995)
How to Find Information – Business: A Guide to Searching in
  Published Sources
London: British Library

This guide provides a comprehensive introduction to finding business information. It lists key texts (printed and CD-ROM), and advice on how they should be used. The British Library also provides a business information service; the address is:

The Business Information Service
25 Southampton Building
London WC2A 1AW
Tel. 020 7412 7498
Fax 020 7412 7453

The following list of sources has been divided into primary and secondary. The main points about each one are explained, together with some detail about their respective advantages and limitations. The amount of information is growing at an alarming rate, so you need to be aware constantly of what is available. Although the details with respect to each of the sources listed were accurate when this book was written, new editions are being published all the time, so do check on publication dates etc. Details of telephone and fax numbers, e-mail addresses and URLs are given where available.

All the indexes, guides and catalogues listed are well known and should be found in most university and large public libraries. A number are published in both paper and CD-ROM versions, and some are available on the Internet. Electronic information sources are growing in number daily, so check what is available before you start to search. Most university libraries run workshops on library and information retrieval skills. Always attend these. Effective library skills are one of the key attributes you need for a successful dissertation.

Primary book sources
This includes conference proceedings, official publications and statistics, patents and trademarks, periodicals, reports, research in progress, standards, theses and trade literature, and these are explained as follows:

CONFERENCE PROCEEDINGS
Business organizations, learned societies, and academic and other associations all hold conferences (also called symposia, congresses, study groups, workshops, colloquia). People run sessions and give talks, and most them are published in special books called proceedings. The information given at conferences is specialized and up-to-date. A large number of conferences are held annually and the best sources to use are:

Index to Conferences Proceedings Received
Boston Spa: British Library Document Supply Centre (BLDSC).

The BIDS service (see page 96) has available the *Index to Scientific and Technical Proceedings (ISTP)*. This index includes papers presented at over 4,000 conferences per year.

These are available at all good academic and university libraries.

OFFICIAL PUBLICATIONS, INCLUDING OFFICIAL STATISTICS

Governments and organizations like the EU and United Nations produce large amounts of information that are very important to all aspects of business. For example, new regulations which can influence trade between nations are being published all the time. The official publications in the UK include Acts of Parliament, command papers and departmental reports. The list is endless, and new publications appear every day. Official publications can provide information which will broaden a topic and help set a dissertation in a national and international context. They are accurate and many include bibliographies which are also good sources of information. Most official publications are given a unique reference number; always quote these accurately when using services like the Inter-Library Loan (ILL) system.

Good sources to trace official publications are:

HMSO Annual Catalogue
London: HMSO.

Catalogue of Official Publications Not Published by HMSO
Cambridge: Chadwyck-Healey.

UKOP: Catalogue of UK Official Publications
This is available on CD-ROM.

If you want to trace EU information, try to find your nearest European Documentation Centre. There are over 50 in the UK and they receive every EU publication. Your university library should be able to inform you of your nearest one. They all have specialist librarians on European matters. There is also a CD-ROM called *CELEX* which is excellent for all EU material.

Official publications, although very good, can be difficult to trace. An excellent guide for UK material is the following:

Butcher, D. (1991)
Official Publications in Britain (2nd edition)
London: Library Association Publishing.

OFFICIAL STATISTICS

In addition to producing reports, Government departments collect data on all aspects of industrial, commercial and domestic life. These are published as official statistics, and it is possible, for example, to find out how many electric kettles were bought in the UK in 1994. It is the Central Statistics Office which collects and collates all the data, and an *Annual Abstract of Statistics* is published. In addition, there are special volumes on social trends and regional trends, which are also worth looking at. The best place to start a search for official statistics is the book *The Guide to Official Statistics*. Look for the most recent edition. It provides details of which statistics are available, both official and unofficial, and how to find them.

PATENTS AND TRADEMARKS

These are sometimes referred to as 'intellectual property'. They are very important in business and may be helpful with dissertations on brand names and marketing. With patents it is possible to carry out a patent analysis which looks at the number and type of patents published over several years in a particular area, e.g. pharmaceuticals. This can be used to show trends and possibly forecast the direction in which research and development should take place. Searching in this whole area can be difficult, but there are a number of good introductory guides:

Newton, D.C. (1991)
Trademarks: An Introductory Guide and Bibliography (2nd edition)
Key Resource Series
London: British Library.

Rimmer, B.M. (updated by van Dulken, D.) (1992)
International Guide to Official Industrial Property Publications (3rd edition)
London: British Library.

van Dulken, D. (1998)
Introduction to Patents Information (3rd edition)
Information in Focus Series
London: British Library.

The Patent Office is a useful contact. The address is:

Concept House
Cardiff Rd
Newport NP9 1RH
Tel. 01633 814000
Fax 01633 814444
e-mail enquiries@patent.gov.uk
http://www.patent.gov.uk

PERIODICALS (ALSO TERMED ACADEMIC JOURNALS)

These form one of the most important types of primary source to use. Most business and management research is published as articles (usually called papers) in academic journals and periodicals. The range is enormous, and there are general titles (e.g. *Management Today*) and very specialized ones (e.g. *Harvard Business Review, Journal of General Management, Journal of Marketing Research*, etc.). Most academic journals have editorial boards which referee and check the papers before they are published, so quality and accuracy are usually guaranteed. Most university libraries hold a range of titles that reflect the research interests of the lecturers. However, as such a large number are published, you should be prepared to use the ILL service.

A good book for tracing business journals is:

> Barrett, D. and Peel, V. (1996)
> *Business Journals at SRIS*
> Key to British Holdings Series
> London: British Library.

A very special type of paper is the literature review, which looks at and summarizes various trends in research that have taken place over a number of years. You have to write a review in your dissertation (see page 138). The main publication which lists journals containing review articles is:

> *Current Serials Received*
> Boston Spa: BLDSC.

REPORTS (INCLUDING MARKET RESEARCH REPORTS)
Reports are an excellent, often under-used, source of information. They are published on all aspects of business and management by government departments, trade associations, academic bodies, special committees, and so on. A good source to search from is:

> *British Reports, Translations and Theses*
> Boston Spa: BLDSC.

Market research reports are very important for business. The British Library holds a large number. A good place to start your search is:

> Leydon, M. and Lee, L. (eds) (1994)
> *Market Research: A Guide to the British Library Collections* (8th edition)
> Key to British Holdings Series
> London: British Library.

RESEARCH IN PROGRESS
Many aspects of research advance so rapidly that it is difficult to keep up-to-date. Also much company information about new products and

services can be confidential. To find out what is happening in academic research the best index to use is:

Current Research in Britain
Boston Spa: BLDSC.

A large number of academics now have home pages on the Internet, so these can also be used.

STANDARDS

Standards are very important in business and may be a helpful place to search if your dissertation involves the service industries. In the UK there is the British Standards Institution (BSI), founded in 1901. The Institute's famous Kitemark is found on everything from power plugs to can openers. There is even a standard on the presentation and layout of dissertations! Standards come in various forms and cover, for example, size, performance, test methods, terminology and codes of practice. The address of the BSI is:

BSI
389 Chiswick High Road
London W4 4AL
Tel. 020 8996 9000
Fax 020 8996 7400

The following book is an excellent introduction to standards information:

Rhodes, J. and Fallone, E. (1998)
Information on Standards: A Guide to Sources
Information in Focus Series
London: published jointly by the British Library and the National
    Library of Scotland.

THESES

This is one of the best places to start a literature search. When postgraduate students are awarded a doctorate PhD degree they are required to deposit a copy of their thesis in their university library, which must be available on the ILL system through the British Library. The thesis is a very specialized academic document, and always contains a literature review on the topic of the research. As theses are assessed by a number of examiners, the quality of the work is always high. Obviously dissertations by undergraduate students do not require the same level of detail as for doctorate students, but if you can find a PhD thesis on a similar topic to your dissertation it will certainly save time in identifying relevant literature. Theses are very easy to trace using the following:

British Reports, Translations and Theses
Boston Spa: BLDSC.

Index to Theses
London: The Association for Information Management (ASLIB).

All publications are available as CD-ROMs. Theses can only be obtained using the ILL service. Because theses have a rarity value (there is usually only one copy in circulation) you may have to read them in your university library. They arrive either as microfilm or microfiche, which need special readers.

TRADE LITERATURE

Industry and commerce produce large quantities of information ranging from leaflets advertising new products to detailed consultancy reports. All of this is termed trade literature and can be very useful in a business dissertation. The main drawback is that the quality varies and most of it is never saved. Old trade literature is difficult to obtain, and the Business Information Service at the British Library is a good place to start. Modern trade literature is easy to get hold of. Simply write to any company or organization you are interested in, and see what they send you. Most libraries have standard catalogues which provide addresses and contact points of British and overseas companies.

Secondary book sources

These include bibliographies, current awareness publications, newspapers, reference books, textbooks and translations.

BIBLIOGRAPHIES

With over 1,000 new books appearing each year in the UK alone, it is very difficult to keep abreast of what is being published. One way is to make regular use of commercial bibliographies. A bibliography is a list of publications, and for each one full details are given. Commercial bibliographies are available which can help if you need to find a general book on a new subject about which you know a little. Most academic libraries keep a number in stock. Two well-known ones are:

British National Bibliography
London: British Library.

British Books in Print (BBIP)
London: J. Whitaker.

Both are available as CD-ROMs. The CD-ROM version of BBIP is called *Bookbank*.

A number of specialized bibliographies are published, for example:

Avery, C. and Zabel, D. (1997)
The Quality Management Sourcebook: An International Guide to Material and Resources
London: Routledge.

Brealey, R. and Edward, H. (1991)
A Bibliography of Finance
London: Massachusetts Institute of Technology Press.

Goodall, F., Gourvish, T. and Tolliday, S. (1997)
International Bibliography of Business History
London: Routledge.

The British Library often commissions bibliographies on special subjects. A recent business one is:

Clough, R. (1995)
Japanese Business Information: An Introduction
Information in Focus Series
London: British Library.

This contains a detailed listing of English language information sources on Japanese business.

CURRENT AWARENESS PUBLICATIONS

With such vast quantities of information being published, it is virtually impossible to keep up-to-date with every new publication. One way to help is to use current awareness publications. Commercial publishers go through all publications extracting details of subjects, authors and other publication information. This data is then re-published either in the form of indexes (publication details only), or abstract (a summary of the work plus publication details). A large number are applicable to business and management, and many of the items listed below are available on-line, in CD-ROM versions and on the Internet. If the electronic forms are available they are quicker to use than the paper versions.

Indexes

There is the *British Humanities Index* and the *Current Technology Index*, both published by the Library Association, London. They cover all UK academic publications, and are well worth a look.

Business Periodical Index. This indexes all English language business periodicals.

Current Contents. Published weekly by the Institute for Scientific Information, Philadelphia, USA, it contains reproductions of the contents pages of all the latest academic journals in most subjects.

Index to Business Reports. This covers over 800 business reports published in business journals and newspapers.

Abstracts
ANBAR. This covers all aspects of business and abstracts over 400 English language journals.

BIDS. This is really excellent and details are given on page 96.

NEWSPAPERS
Newspapers are an important source of business information. They provide public and political opinion, which can be useful to broaden a dissertation. The main newspapers to use are *The Times* and the *Financial Times*. *The Times Index* (also available on CD-ROM) has been published since 1906, and from 1973 included *The Times*, the *Financial Times*, the *Sunday Times* and all the supplements that are published. Other UK national newspapers are available on CD-ROM and these include the *Independent*, the *Telegraph*, the *Mail* and the *Guardian*. For local newspapers ask at your local public library. They often have a clipping service which keeps articles of local interest, new businesses setting up and details of new local major companies.

REFERENCE BOOKS
No library is complete without a selection of standard reference books, such as dictionaries, directories, encyclopedias and so on. The definitive guide to reference publications is *Walford's Guide to Reference Material*. This is a 'classic' book and is readily available in nearly every UK library.

TEXTBOOKS
Textbooks are excellent for providing general background and theory, but a dissertation requires detailed research finding, and up-to-date detail. It is, therefore, advisable to use textbooks sparingly. Make your focus searching out primary material.

TRANSLATIONS
Although English tends to be the main language of business, occasionally you may come across an article in a foreign language. In many instances important work is translated into English, and the following may help to locate a translation:

British Reports, Translations and Theses
Boston Spa: BLDSC.

Journals in Translation
Boston Spa: BLDSC.
This appears irregularly, but lists over 1,000 journals in translation.

Index Translationum: International
Paris: UNESCO.
This lists books which are translated into different languages.

Non-book sources
In addition to traditional forms of information like journals and books, there are other sources that are equally useful in business and management. These include audiovisual material, museums, information about organizations and companies, and people. There are also the electronic forms of information that have become available in recent years.

AUDIOVISUAL MATERIAL
This includes films, videos, tapes, and CDs. Many programmes on television are about business and current affairs and these can provide excellent material for dissertations on topical issues. In addition, a number of films and videos about business issues are published commercially. The following catalogues may help you to find what is available. They should be found in most big libraries:

BUFVC Catalogue
This is the catalogue of the British University Film and Video Council. It lists material published in all British higher education institutions.

British Catalogue of Audio Visual Materials
London: British Library.

British National Film and Video Catalogue
London: British Film Institute.

There is also the National Sound Archive. Part of the British Library, this has a large collection of discs, tapes, films and videos. If you are investigating a particular company, the archive may hold something which could prove useful. The contact address is

> The National Sound Archive
> 29 Exhibition Road
> London SW7 2AS
> Tel. 020 7412 7440

MUSEUMS

If you are researching changes in office layout and associated work practice, a visit to a museum may prove useful. You will be able to see at first hand how the work environment has changed over the years. Museums are excellent storehouses of all types of information, and most of their stock is never put on public display. Many specialize in collecting artefacts about different subjects. A good guide to UK museums is:

> *Museums Year Book Including a Directory of Museums and Galleries of the British Isles*
> London: The Museum Association.

The Museum Association's address is

> The Museum Association
> 43 Clerkenwell Close
> London EC1R 0PA
> Tel. 020 7608 2933
> Fax 020 7250 1929

ORGANIZATIONS, COMPANIES AND INDUSTRIES

Trade associations, industries, companies and other commercial organizations can provide enormous help when preparing dissertations. Most universities have in their reference collections a number of excellent catalogues. The following are especially good:

> Reynard, K.W. and Reynard J.M.E. (eds) (1998)
> *ASLIB Directory of Information Sources in the United Kingdom* (10th edition)
> London: ASLIB.

Henderson, C.A.P. (1998)
Councils, Committees and Boards, Including Government Agencies and Authorities: A Handbook of Advisory, Consultative, Executive, Regulatory and Similar Bodies in British Public Life
Beckenham: CBD Research Ltd.

Henderson, S.P.A. and Henderson, A.J.W. (eds) (1998)
Directory of British Associations and Associations in Ireland (14th edition)
Beckenham: CBD Research Ltd.

Spencer, N. (ed.) (1998)
The Instant Guide to Company Information On-Line: Europe
Key Resource Series
London: British Library.

Key British Enterprises (KBE)
London: Dun & Bradstreet Ltd.

Kompass Register
East Grinstead: Kompass Publishers Ltd.

The International Directory of Business Information Sources and Services (2nd edition) (1996)
London: Europa.

Who Owns Whom?
London: Dun & Bradstreet Ltd.

PEOPLE

People are the best information source available, and if you know someone who can help you, go and see them. Obviously it will be difficult to meet well-known industrialists, politicians, etc. that you might see on television or read about in the newspapers. However, you can always write to them and they may reply, especially if you send a convincing letter about yourself and your dissertation and why you need the information. Famous people can normally be located using *Who's Who*, published by A. & C. Black, London. If you want to contact a researcher or academic whose paper you have read, their addresses are found either at the beginning or end of the paper.

The above list of non-book sources is only a small fraction of what is available. In addition, maps, microfiche, science parks, information services, and news clipping services can all provide extra material. The best advice is to see what is available locally by using your university and local public library.

Electronic information sources
During the last decade electronic information sources have revolutionized research and the process of searching through the literature. For instance, using a computer workstation linked to a CD-ROM can be far more effective and take far less time than sifting through traditional paper versions. Much material is now present in both paper and electronic formats and some publishers now produce certain items only in electronic format. Three examples useful for business are:

Know UK
Cambridge: Chadwyck-Healey.
This is only found on the World Wide Web (WWW) and provides
   information about people and organizations important in the UK.

Periodical Contents Index (PCI)
Cambridge: Chadwyck-Healey.
Available as a CD-ROM and on the WWW, this is an index of over
   2,000 journals in the humanities and social sciences. It covers the
   period from 1770 to 1991.

Research Index
Cambridge: Chadwyck-Healey.
Only on the WWW; it indexes material from business and financial
   journals.

Three electronic formats will be outlined: BIDS, CD-ROMs and the WWW (and Internet). Access may be restricted unless you have the correct user-IDs and passwords – ask at your local library.

BIDS (BATH INFORMATION AND DATA SERVICES)
BIDS provides access to three multi-disciplinary citation indexes (Science Citation Index, Social Science Citation Index and the Arts and Humanities Citation Index). A citation index is a listing by author of the references given at the end of a paper, together with a list of authors who have quoted (or cited) them. BIDS also has incorporated into its database the Scientific and Technical Proceedings (ISTP) index. The data for BIDS is supplied and owned by the Institute of Scientific Information Inc. USA. Over 7,000 journals, in all subjects, are indexed and the information is updated weekly, so BIDS is always current. BIDS is available in all large libraries.

BIDS is an extremely versatile and efficient information searching tool. If it's available, then use it. It is one the best retrieval systems on the market. You can search in a number of ways, by keywords, author, paper title and research topic. Although it does not provide full text of the items traced, it will certainly alert you to what's available. References are printed on the screen and can also be downloaded onto a disc.

CD-ROMS

CD-ROM stands for compact disc read only memory and is another very efficient electronic information system. Looking like a music CD each CD-ROM can store text, pictures and graphs, and one disc holds the equivalent of 250,000 pages of printed text. Some CD-ROMs store full text and others only have abstracts with full bibliographical details. As with BIDS, the information can be downloaded if required. The number on the market is increasing all the time. The following list is good for business and management, and some of the titles have already been listed, as many publishers now produce the printed and the CD versions. All are well known, so only the titles are given:

ABI Inform
This gives access to over 1,000 academic, management, marketing and business journals.

American Humanities Index
Similar to the *British Humanities Index*, this covers American journals.

Index to Theses

ASSIA (Applied Social Sciences Index and Abstracts)

Bookbank

British Humanities Index

Dissertation Abstracts

European Business

FAME (Financial Analysis Made Easy)
This contains facts and figures about 110,000 major public and private British companies – up to 5 years' financial detail is given.

Key British Enterprises

Kompass

MCB Emerald
This contains full-text versions of a number of journals in most
aspects of business and management.

UK Company Factfinder

UKOP
Also on the WWW, this has details of British official publications
and publications of organizations like UNESCO.

A number of UK newspapers are also on CD-ROM: the *Independent*,
the *Mail*, the *Daily Telegraph*, the *Guardian* and *The Times*.

THE WORLD WIDE WEB (WWW) AND THE INTERNET
The Internet is a world-wide computer network that offers instant
access to thousands of computer files. Part of the Internet is JANET
(Joint Academic Network) – this links throughout the UK universities,
colleges and research organizations. The Internet is the infrastructure
which supports the WWW. This is a set of files and each file has a
unique address termed a uniform resource locator (URL). Without
going into very much technical detail the files are accessed by what is
known as a browser (e.g. Netscape Navigator, Microsoft Explorer). If
you don't know which file to access you can use a search engine (e.g.
Altavista, Yahoo, Excite, etc.) which provides both subject and keyword
search facilities.

The Internet and WWW are relatively new, a vast amount of
information is available and it is changing all the time. It is also easy
to access. However, because it is new, much of the material lacks
academic credibility and you need to use your judgement when
accessing some of the information available. You must cite electronic
sources in your dissertation as with any other source. Details on this
are given on page 145.

With so much material on the WWW the following list is only the
tip of the iceberg, and the current URL for each source listed is given.

Journal articles
  Searchbank
  A full-text database of journal articles from academic and trade
    journals. It can be found at www.searchbank.com/searchbank

  Proquest
  This is a full-text database from business journals and magazines. It
    can be found at http://www.umi.com/pqdauto

Newspapers
> The *Financial Times* can be found at http://www.ft.com/

Company information
> Lots of well-known companies now have home pages, for example
> Marks & Spencer plc can be found at
> http://www.marks-and-spencer.co.uk/

Directories
> *UK Business Directory*
> This gives addresses of over 50,000 companies. It can be found at
> http://www.milfac.co.uk/milfac/

Associations
> Institute of Management. It can be found at
> http://www.inst-mgt.org.uk

NEWSGROUPS AND DISCUSSION LISTS

If you have an e-mail address on the Internet you can join newsgroups and discussion lists. They can be found using the search engines. Remember, the amount of information circulating on the Net is enormous so take care when using it for your dissertation.

Libraries and business information

All libraries, even small ones, need to organize and keep accurate records of their stock. The stock is very varied, and as well as books, periodicals and videos, libraries now house CD-ROMs and other electronic information sources. In recent years the role of many university libraries has changed, and in addition to providing books they are now a centre for IT and other learning support material. However, libraries still need to keep a complete record of their material and this is termed the *catalogue*. How the stock is arranged is called the *classification system*, and the exact location where all items on the same subject may be found is called the *class mark*. Libraries classify their stock using different systems. One of the first things you need to do is to get to know how your libraries work in terms of their catalogue and classification systems. Most libraries now have their catalogue computerized, although some of their older stock may still be recorded on index cards.

A computerized catalogue enables searching to be carried out very quickly, and most systems allow searching by book title, author or subject. The subject search facility often allows you to search by keyword. That is a search for a particular word, or set of words, found in the title of a book. An example of a keyword search would be 'management by objectives'. Any book in the library with these words in the title would be displayed on the computer screen. Some systems even indicate the number of items in stock, and whether a particular book is out on loan, or reserved for another reader, or available in the library. You may also obtain a print-out and this can save time writing down book details.

Classification systems

All library classification systems divide knowledge into major areas, which in turn are sub-divided a number of times until all items on the same subject are placed together. University libraries use, in the main, one of two systems to classify their stock. They are the Dewey decimal system and the Library of Congress system. Each will be briefly described.

THE DEWEY DECIMAL SYSTEM

This was originally devised by M. Dewey (1851–1931). The system divides knowledge into 10 classes:

    000 – Generalities
    100 – Philosophy and Related Disciplines
    200 – Religion
    300 – Social Sciences
    400 – Language
    500 – Pure Sciences
    600 – Technology (Applied Sciences)
    700 – The Arts and Recreation
    800 – Literature
    900 – General Geography, History and their Auxiliaries

Each category is then separated into 10 divisions, numbering 0–9. Division 0 is for general works and 1–9 for the different subjects within a major area. The difficulty with business and management is that by nature it is very wide in terms of subject. For example, Economics, an important part of business, is classified at 330 in the 300s under the Social Sciences, while many other aspects of management are classified in the 600s under Technology. The majority of business and management books are in the 650s. For example:

    651 – Office Systems
    657 – Accounting

658 – General Management
659 – Advertising and Public Relations

Each division can be divided further. For example, 658, which is General Management, includes

658.3 – Personnel (HRM)
658.4 – Executive Management
658.5 – Management of Production

Each of the above can be sub-divided even further, for example 658.4

658.42 – Top Management
658.43 – Middle Management

The advantage with the Dewey system is that it is very flexible and allows for very small divisions and small, discrete subjects can be classified easily.

LIBRARY OF CONGRESS SYSTEM
This was devised by H. Putman in 1897 for the Library of Congress in Washington, DC in the United States. It is a more complicated system than Dewey and knowledge is split into 21 areas, each one represented by a letter. Business is found at the letter H, which includes all the social sciences. The letter H is then followed by a second letter, which indicates subject areas. For example, HB is where Economics is classified, and HF, which is known as Commerce, is where business and management items are found. The subject divisions within general areas are indicated by numbers. For example, HF 5001–6182 is where Business and Business Administration is classified. The mix of letters and numbers makes this system more difficult to use.

OTHER CLASSIFICATION SYSTEMS
Other systems exist, e.g. the BLISS system and Universal Decimal System (UDS). These can be found in specialized libraries which house unique collections of material.

Specialized library services
Libraries offer specialized services, such as the Inter-Library Loan (ILL) service, which allows books to be borrowed from other libraries. Some libraries are copyright libraries, e.g. the British Library, and by law they receive copies of everything published in the UK. Most university libraries offer services like short loan and one week loan services. Enquire what is available locally. The following two books are excellent guides to show you what is available within UK libraries:

Dale, P. (ed.) (1993)
Guide to Libraries in Key UK Companies
Key Resource Series
London: British Library.
This guide helps you access some of the best special libraries in industries found in UK top business and industrial companies. It lists over 200 specialist libraries.

Dale, P. (ed.) (1998)
Guide to Libraries and Information Units in Government Departments and Other Organisations (33rd edition)
Key Resource Series
London: British Library.
This is a classic reference book, and provides information on over 700 libraries and similar collections in the UK. It lists the European Documentation Centres mentioned on page 86.

Guidelines on making a literature search

Having a working knowledge of the various sources available is essential if your literature searching is to be effective. As identified earlier, as you collect information, you must read it through and constantly evaluate it. The following scheme is suggested for beginning a literature search.

- *Define your topic.* Clearly define what you want to search for. Make a preliminary selection of major books and review articles. Good sources to use at this stage are indexes, abstracts, theses and reports. Use electronic versions if available as they are quicker and more detailed. As far as possible, access primary sources. At this stage, have your dissertation proposal handy. In preparing the proposal you will have already begun to search the literature.

- *Decide on keyword and search terms.* Most indexes and abstracts use keyword and search terms. Decide on suitable words or terms for your dissertation. A quick brainstorm at this stage will help. For example, if you were searching the role of teams and team building, the search terms you look for could include the following words connected with teams: cohesion, competition, formation, ideal teams, effective teams, high performance teams, self-managing teams, team building skills, barriers to team building. If your dissertation is concerned with team building skills in relation to an IT company, you would look for examples specifically linking IT and teams. As you identify the various references, quickly scan the material to ensure it is the sort of thing you need. If not, then start again with a new set of keywords. Effective literature searching is an iterative process and one good reference will start to lead to others.

- *Identify the best sources to use.* As stated earlier, the emphasis should be on using primary sources, and as you begin to collect the sort of material you want, particular journal titles and authors will crop up a number of times. If you locate a particularly good reference, e.g. a research paper, look at the bibliography listed. This may also provide useful sources.

- *Supplement the information collected from other sources.* Once you are into the literature search, remember sources like newspapers, companies, trade associations and official publications. They can often provide an extra dimension and will give extra information to supplement the more detailed material found in research articles.

- *Record and evaluate the material.* Always keep meticulous records of every source used. You need these details for your dissertation's bibliography. How to set out a bibliography is described on pages 142–5. When reading the material, look for the useful quotation you may need to include when writing up. Evaluating material is very important and is explained in more detail in the next section.

Evaluating the information

Collecting the correct information is only the first step – how you use the information is equally important. Making notes and simply summarizing the information collected and arranging it into chronological order does not constitute evaluation. You will need to identify trends, develop themes, compare one reference with another, and establish links with the accepted theories of your subject. Evaluation is really important, and when the author holds workshops on dissertations, this area of work is emphasized. It is one of the most important aspects of dissertation work.

The following pointers may help you get the best from the material you collect:

- *How does the information relate to your dissertation?* Always relate the material to the objectives of your investigation. Whatever you read, be it a chapter from a book, thesis, report or article in a journal, ask yourself, 'Why am I reading this reference? Do I want a summary of the topic, or isolated examples to back up and provide evidence to support a particular point?' Never read anything without an objective in mind. Obviously when you are just beginning your literature search you will need to read most material to get yourself acquainted with the topic. However, after the very early stages, read everything with a critical and discerning eye looking for particular information – be selective!

- *The basic questions you should ask.* Dissertations should be critical and analytical, not merely descriptive. This approach can start at the literature stage by asking some basic questions like 'Why?', 'What?', 'When?', 'Where?' and 'How?' about the information you collect.

- *Date and age of material.* Just because material is old does not mean it's no good. The basics may be just as valid as when first published and only the examples need to be more up-to-date. Many of the laws and principles of science still hold true today; it is the understanding and interpretation that have changed over time.

- *Primary versus secondary material.* There is a very important difference between primary and secondary material (see page 84). Primary sources contain information which is new at the time of publication; secondary sources contain material which is second-hand and has been published before. For research purposes, greater reliance can be placed on primary sources. It would be unwise to base a dissertation entirely on secondary sources like textbooks.

- *Reliance – description versus discussion and fact versus opinion.* It is important to gauge how much you can rely on the information you collect. Ask yourself whether you are reading fact, opinion, description or discussion. You may read that 'London is a wonderful capital city'. It is a fact that London is a capital city, but whether it is wonderful depends on your understanding and meaning of the word 'wonderful', and if you think this description applies to cities. You may well need opinion and it is a very useful exercise to include a comparison of different researchers' opinions. However, it is essential, when evaluating library material, to recognize whether what you read is based on empirical research and evidence, opinion or just a bright idea.

- *Where did the author get the information from?* Very few academic writers rely entirely on their own ideas for the basis of their writing. Most use other people's work. Look at the number and type of references quoted in the things you read. An extensive and wide-ranging list of sources indicates that the writer has been thorough in searching out material. A short list may indicate a somewhat superficial look at the subject. Always go through any reference list – you may identify other useful information sources that are worth chasing up.

- *How did the author collect the information and is it reliable?* If the material contains details of, for example, experiments, interviews, and questionnaires, ask yourself how reliable the results are. Would you believe the results of a survey based on a sample size of less than 10 people? If the author has used any quantitative methods, are the calculations correct and have tests of significance been used? Academics can make mistakes like anyone else! If the researcher has used qualitative techniques, do you agree with the way the concepts and ideas have been identified as a result of the research? Do you think the researcher has made short cuts which could invalidate some of the findings? Always be prepared to ask questions.

- *Can you adapt, change, repeat a methodology in either another context or with another example?* Don't be afraid to use someone else's method or approach. Provided you fully acknowledge their work it is not plagiarism. In fact, carrying out a similar piece of work in a different context may help validate both their work and yours. It provides a ready-made comparison and this gives a good starting point when you come to write up your dissertation.

- *Can any published data you find be reworked to reveal new trends and new insights?* Often by reworking data you may reveal new trends and ideas. For example, arranging a table of data into a graph or chart may help you understand it much better. Descriptions of processes and long detailed accounts can often be drawn as diagrams such as flowcharts. In fact, anything that helps your understanding and appreciation will be useful.

A final word

This chapter has looked at the information needs of a dissertation. It is an area that is tremendously important. Effective information retrieval and evaluation skills are essential and they should become research tools in their own right.

8   Evaluating research results

Introduction

You have spent a great deal of effort and time collecting your research results. They may be in the form of completed questionnaires, transcripts of interviews and focus groups, diaries, or experimental data. In fact, you may have results from a whole range of research techniques. You now have to sift through and interpret them, and this forms a major part of your final dissertation. Irrespective of whether you have qualitative or quantitative results, you must relate the findings to the original aims of the dissertation. This may be a somewhat obvious point to make, but very often in dissertations the interpretation of the research evidence bears little relevance to the research question carefully set up at the start and identified in the original proposal. It is a good idea at the interpretation stage to keep a copy of the proposal handy. It is also essential to recollect whether the data is quantitative or qualitative, as this will govern aspects of the analysis. Table 8.1 summarizes the essential differences between quantitative and qualitative data.

It is helpful at this stage to review the research approach and methods, and revise why they were selected. What were their relative advantages and limitations? How did the literature inform your research design? Were any special concepts and ideas identified in the literature and, if so, can they be used at this interpretation stage?

This chapter offers suggestions on how to analyse and interpret your research results. Sections are devoted to quantitative and qualitative research. There are, however, a number of general points which apply equally to both approaches and these are explained first.

General points about the interpretation of research results

Research produces a lot of results and, as they stand, they can be unwieldy, so you need to reduce the amount of material collected. The

Table 8.1 Comparison of quantitative and qualitative data

Quantitative data	Qualitative data
Based on meanings derived from numbers. The data may be nominal (categorical), ordinal, interval or ratio.	Meaning is expressed in words.
Collection of data is numerical and in standardized form.	Collection of data is non-standardized and uses a variety of formats.
Analysis is by the use of tables, diagrams and statistical methods. The methods used depend on whether the data is nominal (categorical), ordinal, interval or ratio.	Analysis is via the use of descriptions and the identification of concepts.

reduction of data is very important in the process of interpretation. It must be done, however, without losing sense or order. Techniques such as tables, figures, flowcharts, the listing of categories, the identification of themes and ideas all help to cut down the amount of paper and material you are handling.

As you reduce the amount of paper, look for themes, ideas and concepts which may emerge. Try to identify overarching and broad propositions which may join a number of ideas together. Are they linked in any special way? Are particular relationships emerging? As you work through the data try to separate it into its component parts. Look for reasons to explain the results.

Don't ignore the literature review at this stage. It can provide useful clues. Is your data, for example, similar to that which other people have produced before? Do your ideas agree or disagree with those of other researchers? Try and build what some people term conceptual frameworks.

When working through the results constantly refer back to the way you collected them. These two factors are intrinsically linked. Have your chosen techniques proven successful and the most suitable? With hindsight would you repeat the work in exactly the same way, or make changes? A critique of your methodology in the light of the results is important. Research is not just about collecting results; the appropriateness of how you collected them is just as important. Be reflective during the whole process of data interpretation. Self-reflection is an important aspect of contemporary management research. It helps to establish your views and opinions about the topic, and whether or not they have changed during the duration of the research.

Guard against simply summarizing and providing a précis of your results. Without thinking, researchers describe their results, assuming that description equates to interpretation. It does not. Interpretation shows how your results fit, or do not fit, with the theory and background of the subject investigated. Don't be afraid to challenge and question accepted practice. If your methodology and techniques have a strong rationale and indicate a particular line of argument, then be bold and say so. It is the strength of your argument that is important.

Finally, there is no standard approach to analysing research results. This distinguishes research, especially in such broad areas as business and management. Don't be afraid to look for something new and different. A good and analytical interpretation will make your work stand out.

Qualitative data analysis

Qualitative research always generates lots of material. This now has to be gone through and some sense made of it all. Although you were advised at the collection stage to think about the processes of interpretation, in reality this is difficult to do. At the end there always seems a large bulk of material to interpret.

The following procedure for the analysis of qualitative data is suggested:

- Read through all result formats, e.g. interview transcripts, questionnaires, observation sheets, etc. As you work through, carefully note down any points and ideas that are identified.
- Go through each different type of format a second time and identify in each one what you consider to be the definitive list of ideas and topics mentioned. Give each discrete topic a code, e.g. a number or letter, so it can be identified at a later date. The overall aim is to end up with, for example in an interview transcript, the format marked up with different letters and numbers, each one representing a separate idea. Don't forget to write down what each number or letter stands for. For instance, if the dissertation was on decision-making, you might identify from your interviews

the following ideas, each of which could be given a code as follows:

Idea	Code
Team work in decision-making	D1
Explanation of a good decision	D2
Explanation of a bad decision	D3
How to make decisions	D4
Conditions necessary to make effective decisions	D5

- As you work through your material, you may decide to include extra categories. For instance, with the above example you may begin to identify behavioural aspects of decision-making and this in turn may be sub-divided into subjects like attitude, emotions, gender, intuition, etc. It is essential that you constantly reflect back to check that ideas have not been missed. Some people, at this stage, actually cut up the interview transcript and sort each idea into individual files. If you decide to do this, give each separate piece of paper its own identification number, so that if you need to you can re-assemble them back into their original format. Depending on how many pieces of paper you have, making a photocopy of each sheet prior to cutting up could save time. As you work through the material you may come across useful quotes given by your interviewees or respondents, which seem to summarize an idea that you have identified. Keep a special note of these. When writing up, a succinct quote used at an appropriate point will certainly hammer home your line of argument.
- Finally, when all the results have been assigned to a particular category, you then need to go back and re-read all the comments with respect to one idea. This is the stage when patterns begin to emerge and the real interpretation begins. You may be able to link some of the ideas with those already identified in the literature. It may be possible to convert some of the qualitative data into a quantitative format. For example, can you calculate the percentage frequency of a particular idea, and give an estimate of its occurrence?

The above method of analysis takes considerable time, and you need to be meticulous so that you can re-trace your steps if required. In summary, you have accomplished two things:

- You have gone through all your results and data collection records and divided them up into representative categories and ideas.
- By doing this you have identified how these can be linked to form larger and more general themes. You have begun the process of conceptualization.

The above scheme is general, but should suit most undergraduate dissertations. There are, however, some special techniques of qualitative data analysis. These include, for example, *content analysis*, where the frequency of keywords and concepts is calculated. It is really a more sophisticated version of what has been described here. Another technique uses the concept of *grounded theory*, and this is now described.

The role of grounded theory

The idea of grounded theory was first identified by Glaser and Strauss (1967). It has spread to all areas of qualitative research, and is the outcome of inductive research. It is theory that arises from the data collected by empirical research. A great deal has been written about it, and in many cases the original ideas of Glaser and Strauss have become altered. An excellent summary of their work is given in Denscombe (1998). The essential points about grounded theory are as follows.

It is in the main a pragmatic approach. Qualitative research can be very different in that at the start no observable patterns in the data may be apparent. Too prescribed an approach can be counter-productive, failing to take on board all the complexities of what qualitative research is; it is a descriptive process. Qualitative research, it is argued, should not simply describe a situation, but look for explanations and analyses, and at all levels a search should be made for generalizations or theories to explain and understand the topic being investigated. These generalizations or theories should, therefore, emerge or be 'grounded' in the empirical research. Hence the term 'grounded theory'. Implicit in the process is that the researcher constantly looks back and reflects, and as a result refines the theory against new research findings.

With grounded theory the researcher must have an open mind right from the start. Pre-conceived ideas about a situation should be ignored. It is here that a problem arises. It is very difficult for any researcher to put aside thoughts about a subject. It is important to emphasize that an open mind does not equate to an empty one. If you intend to take a grounded theory approach, the literature still needs reviewing, and a working knowledge of the topic being investigated is required.

The following is a suggested grounded theory scheme of analysis.

It is similar to the scheme already described to analyse qualitative data, in that patterns and themes are identified. The difference is that with a grounded theory approach you treat the material as a whole (i.e. holistically) while attempting to explore the meaning and context of the data.

The suggested scheme is:

- *Familiarization with material.* Here you read and re-read the work, teasing out patterns and themes. In particular, search for nuances and attitudes, and get a feel for the material.

- *Reflection.* At this stage you ask questions such as 'Does the research data support existing knowledge?', 'Does it challenge existing knowledge?', 'Does it answer previously unanswered questions?', and 'If the data is different, why is it different?'

- *Conceptualization.* Here you identify patterns and concepts that begin to emerge from the data. As in the method described above, the use of letters and numbers to code material may help.

- *Cataloguing concepts.* The identified concepts are now recorded on index cards (or computer database). Each entry contains full details of where the same concept occurs.

- *Linking.* The ideas are now linked together and hopefully you start to build the grounded theory. At this stage areas may be identified where there is a shortage of material, so you may need to revisit your original data to ensure that no important point is missed, or you may decide to collect more data should the time allow.

The use of grounded theory is popular in certain areas of human resource management and in investigations which look at the cultural concepts of an organization.

Computers and qualitative data

In recent years, computer software has been developed to aid in the analysis of qualitative data. A well-known example is NUDIST (non-numerical unstructured data, indexing, searching, theorizing). The program is extremely versatile and can be used in a number of ways. It does, however, take time to input the data and some expertise is necessary to get the best out of the package. Computer programs take away some of the tedious sorting and sifting. They also help with coding and categorizing material, and at the end you have the original data still left in one piece, where manual methods require you to divide it up. Although the programs can code, retrieve, search, index and take out a lot of the drudgery, the final interpretation is still left up to the researcher, you.

Quantitative data analysis

In many ways the analysis and interpretation of quantitative data is similar to that of qualitative data. The same principles apply, in that the data must be reduced in bulk to make it more manageable. What concerns many students with quantitative data is the use of statistics and the associated mathematical formulae involved. Fortunately, there are now software packages available to lessen the mathematical burden. It is important to note that statistics does not always imply long and complicated calculations.

This section works through a number of different areas associated with the handling of quantitative results. It looks at the preparation of data for analysis, sometimes called coding, and the use of both descriptive and inferential statistics.

Descriptive statistics involves describing and displaying results in the form of tables and diagrams, such as bar charts and pie charts. Arithmetical calculations are also part of descriptive statistics, but in the main they are straightforward and used to measure the dispersion (i.e. the spread of a distribution) of the data. Inferential statistics is more mathematically demanding and involves the concepts of probability, and the carrying out of mathematical tests of significance.

An understanding of the basics involved in statistics is needed, so that you will appreciate which type can be used in different research situations. It is important to think about the use of statistics at the start of your research. When used correctly, they are a very useful research tool. However, when wrongly applied, they only weaken results and can present a misleading picture of the research.

This section aims to provide an overview on the use of statistics. Detailed mathematical formulae are not given; the Bibliography lists useful books should you want more detail.

Preparing quantitative data for analysis

Quantitative analysis requires the data to be in the form of numbers. This is an obvious statement to make, but if you decide to use any type of quantitative data collection you need to think at the start how the data, if not collected in number form, can be transposed into numbers. With interviews and questionnaires, for example, the raw information is mostly in the form of descriptions, or ticks in boxes. You need to transfer these into numbers. This is called *coding*. It is achieved by working through the interview transcripts, questionnaires, etc. and allocating each separate idea or concept identified a numerical code. Use the pilot studies carried out early in the research to decide on the form of coding. This can save a great deal of time later on.

Let's take an example of coding. Suppose you are carrying out an awareness survey of senior managers about business process re-engineering, and are using a questionnaire as the main method of collecting data. The first question might read as follows:

Before receiving this questionnaire were you already aware of business process re-engineering?

Please tick appropriate box	Yes	0
	No	1

The response 'Yes' is given the numerical value of 0, and 'No' is given the numerical value of 1. When you have received all the returned questionnaires, go through the replies and count the total number of 0s and the total number of 1s. You can then go on to calculate the percentage frequencies. The question asked above is termed a closed question, in that only one type of response can be recorded, 'Yes' or 'No'.

Some questions can be described as partly open, in that the respondents are given a range of potential answers. For example:

Where did you first hear about business process re-engineering?

Radio	0
TV	1
Newspaper	2
Trade journal	3
Other source(s)	4
Don't know	5

Please tick appropriate box

If you have ticked other source(s) please state source(s)

_____

_____

Under the heading 'other sources' the respondent could state, for example, conference, meeting with colleagues, the Internet, or attending a training programme. You need to work through all the returned questionnaires and list all the different sources identified and code them, e.g. conference would be 6, meeting with colleagues 7, the Internet 8, attending a training programme 9, and so on. As with the first example you could calculate percentage frequencies, etc.

Coding completely open questions is more difficult and time-consuming. Using the business process re-engineering example, an open question might read 'What factors govern the success or otherwise of business process re-engineering?' To answer a question like this respondents have to list their perceived reasons, or may write one or two sentences explaining their views. Here you need to work through each questionnaire, looking for discrete comments made by the respondents. Having identified all the possible replies you then code them, with the first concept being 0 and so on until every separate idea has a number. Coding open questions reflects the judgement of the researcher. In the early stages try to use as many categories of response as possible. The number can always be reduced at a later stage, and what at first might appear separate categories can be linked.

Coding is a tedious and time-consuming business and you need to double-check, particularly with open questions, that you are being consistent and applying the correct codes. Often respondents may express the same idea, but use different words. It is important that every type of code is independent and mutually exclusive of one another. As stated earlier, it is a good idea to sort the coding out at the pilot stage, and then the questionnaires can often be coded (i.e. pre-coded) before they are distributed.

Quantitative analysis and computers
Very sophisticated and powerful software packages are now available, e.g. Minitab, SPSS and Sigtest. The majority of them are written to provide a number of functions, and once the data is input, a number of different tests and calculations can be made. They will set out and draw tables, graphs and charts. Some packages even allow for missing values and unanswered questions on a questionnaire. As with any package, practise with your pilot data.

Descriptive statistics

Diagrams and tables are an excellent way to describe and compare data. For instance, a table can augment an account of a survey, and a well-labelled flowchart can be used to add to a description of an industrial process. General advice about the use of tables and diagrams is given. This is followed with a range of examples.

- In text the tables are referred to as tables, and diagrams like charts and graphs are collectively called figures. Both are numbered using Arabic numbers, and the numbers should correspond to those given in the text. The numbering should incorporate the section of the dissertation where the table or figure is found (e.g. Figure 3.4 is the fourth figure in Chapter 3).
- Tables and figures should always be large and neatly produced, whether drawn by hand or computer. They should be given a self-explanatory title, and if you are using someone else's material, they should be referenced as with any other cited information.
- When using numbers always state the units. Big numbers can be shortened, e.g. 18,000,000 can be shown as 1.8×10^7. If levels of statistical significance are used they must either be incorporated in the title or given as a footnote.
- Don't overcrowd a table with too much information, as it will be less easy to read.
- Don't let tables and figures stand alone. Do refer to them in the writing summarizing the main points for the reader. Good figures and tables add to the written text, they do not replace it.

Tables

Tables are usually used to display numbers and since they are arranged in columns and rows the numbers can be easily compared; this will help to reveal trends and patterns. As actual numbers are quoted, tables are more precise than figures, and the reader can identify particular values. Table 8.2 is an example of a table using numbers. It is taken from Lowe and Gilligan (1995) who carried out research on SMEs and the table shows the type of information SMEs needed. The table also compares the percentage of companies obtaining the information from either public agencies or private consultancies.

There are also non-numerical tables and Table 8.3 is an example of one. It lists certain well-known management writers, sometimes referred to as the gurus of management, and includes some of their ideas.

Table 8.2 Percentage of companies that have sought help on the following topics from public agencies and private consultancies (n=135)

Type of information needed	% seeking help from the public agencies	% seeking help from private consultancies
Start up	16	27
Finance	23	49
Business planning	19	39
Marketing	22	22
Exporting	13	9
Business information	21	21
Quality	15	21
Technology	11	10
Health & Safety	23	19
Recruitment	20	16

Source: Lowe and Gilligan (1995)

Table 8.3 Well-known management gurus and their respective ideas

Writer	Idea
Chandler, A.D.	Decentralization
de Bono, E.	Lateral Thinking
Drucker, P.	Management by Objectives
Kanter, R.M.	Empowerment
Juran, J.	Company-wide Quality Management
McGregor, D.	Theory X and Theory Y
Maslow, A.	Motivation: Hierarchy of Needs
Porter, M.	Competitive Strategy
Revans, R.	Action Learning
Taylor, F.W.	Scientific Management

Source: Kennedy (1993)

Figures

Figures are not as precise as tables, but do have more visual impact and are an excellent means of illustrating data. The following selection gives some idea of the range of techniques that can be used to display information in figure format. The list is by no means complete and it is worth keeping your eye on publications like *The Financial Times* and *Which*. They both present data in novel and interesting ways. The main point to note is that figures like graphs and histograms have certain mathematical properties, so only use them if you understand the theory involved.

Graphs

A graph is an excellent way to illustrate the relationship between two sets of results (known as variables). The line drawn on the graph represents this relationship. It indicates how a change in one relates to a change in the other. Figure 8.1 is an example of a graph and shows the relationship between the number of sales in the dissertation department store over time. The horizontal axis of the graph is termed the x axis (the abscissa) and the vertical axis is termed the y axis (the ordinate). The independent variable is plotted on the horizontal axis, which in this example is time, and the dependent variable on the vertical axis, here the number of purchasers. The axes should always start at 0 and this is termed the origin of the graph. In most examples time is the independent variable, but not in every case. A clue in recognizing the two variables is to examine the results being plotted. The independent variable changes at regular intervals, while the dependent variable is more erratic and irregular. Figure 8.2 shows the various parts of the graph.

Many software packages now construct graphs. However, when constructing a graph always use a sensible scale for both axes. Excessive manipulation of data can make the graph look strange and is often misleading. The vertical axis must always start at 0, so if the dependent

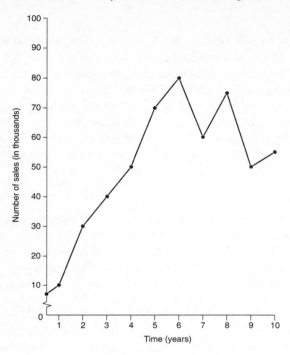

Figure 8.1 Graph showing number of sales in the dissertation department store over a 10-year period

Note: The y axis (the dependent variable) has been broken with a zigzag line because of the magnitude of the scale.

scale is long it is permissible to break the axis by a zigzag line. It is also possible to plot several lines on one graph. In Figure 8.1, two lines could have been plotted, one representing male shoppers, the other female shoppers.

As stated above, graphs have mathematical properties, and it is possible in certain situations to transpose the data and plot a different type of graph. An example is the semi-log graph. Here the results for the dependent variable (y axis) are plotted as log numbers, while the results for the independent variable (x axis) are left unchanged. This results in a semi-log graph, and these can be useful to compare rates of sales of two similar products.

Other graphs used in business are the Z chart and Lorenz curves. The Z chart is a graph that represents only one year's data, and incorporates within it monthly totals (again of a particular product), monthly

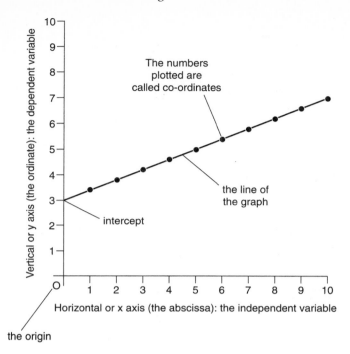

Figure 8.2 Diagram showing the various parts of a graph

Note: Scales and units on both axes are arbitrary.
Source: Adapted from White (1991)

cumulated figures for the year and a moving annual total. The graph is called a Z chart because when all the numbers are graphed they look like the letter Z. Lorenz curves are very specialized, and used to show inequality. For example, it is usually accepted that in every country a small portion of the population owns and controls a large proportion of the wealth. Lorenz curves may be used, therefore, in situations where the incomes present in the population are being studied and industrial output and efficiency are also being measured. Graphs can become mathematically complicated. Only take them as far as you understand them.

Pie charts
Pie charts are easily understood by the reader, and simple to construct. White (1991) gives instructions on how to do it by hand if you don't have a software package available. The word pie comes from the fact that a circle is divided up into slices, like a cake or pie. The whole circle represents the whole sample and it is divided according to the size of

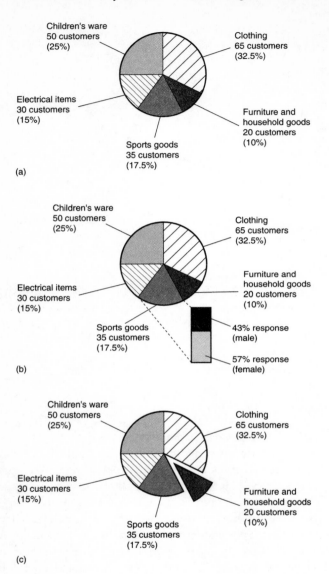

Figure 8.3 Different examples of pie chart layouts using data from Table 8.4

(a) Standard pie chart.

(b) With this layout a percentage bar chart is added to one sector to show the ratio of male to female customers.

(c) With this layout one sector has been pulled away from the pie. This is useful if you want to emphasize one particular sector.

each component part. Pie charts can be used as an alternative to bar charts and there are a number of variations in their construction. It is possible to combine the pie chart with the percentage bar chart, if one sector of the pie is especially interesting. Figure 8.3 shows a number of different pie chart layouts all using the same data taken from Table 8.4. Don't divide the chart into too many sectors: four or five is usually enough.

Table 8.4 First purchase by a random sample of 200 customers in the dissertation department store on 1 January 1999

Department	Male	Female	Total
Clothing	20	45	65
Children's ware	20	30	50
Furniture & household goods	10	10	20
Sports goods	15	20	35
Electrical items	18	12	30
Total number in sample			**200**

Bar charts
Bar charts are like graphs in that they have data on two axes, but on one axis the variable is non-numerical. Figure 8.4 shows a range of different bar chart formats, all using data from Table 8.4. This data was also used in the pie chart examples.

Histograms
These are not bar charts, but specialized diagrams to show frequency distributions. If we take the same 200 customers at the dissertation department store, but this time record in km how far they have travelled to the shop, the distribution would be as set out in Table 8.5.

When drawn out in the form of a chart, as in Figure 8.5, the data is termed a histogram. It is important to note that histograms have mathematical properties, in that the area of each column is proportional to the frequency of each class. This means if one class has a frequency twice that of another, then the area of the respective column will also be twice as much. It is important to note that a histogram plots data that is continuous. In the example given people can travel any distance to arrive at the shop. Therefore, when drawing out the histogram all the blocks touch one another. Frequency distributions which plot discrete data are called column graphs.

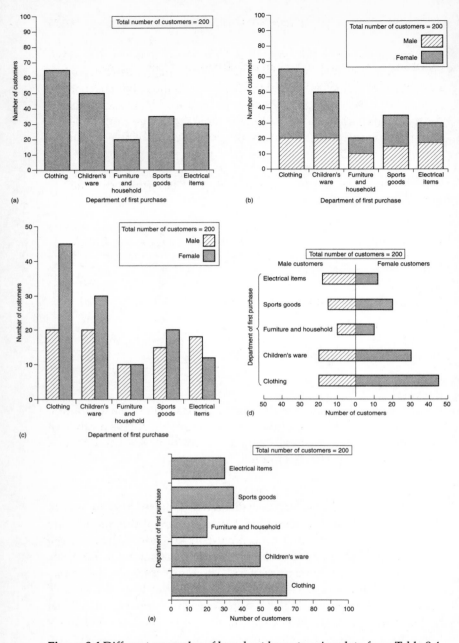

Figure 8.4 Different examples of bar chart layouts using data from Table 8.4

(a) A vertical bar chart. (b) A component bar chart. (c) A multiple bar chart. (d) A back to back (or change) bar chart. (e) A horizontal bar chart. This is useful if a large number of bars is needed; it is easy to extend the vertical scale.

Table 8.5 Distances travelled in km by 200 customers visiting the dissertation department store

Number of km travelled to reach the store	Number of customers
0 – under 5	10
5 – under 10	45
10 – under 15	70
15 – under 20	55
20 – under 25	14
25 – under 30	6
Total number of customers	**200**

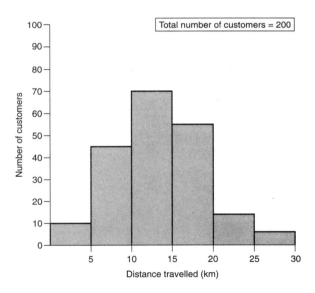

Figure 8.5 An example of a histogram showing the frequency of customers and the distance travelled to the dissertation department store (based on data in Table 8.5)

Column graphs

If we look at our dissertation store data once again, but this time ask the customers how many times they have visited the shop in the previous six months, the data might be as set out in Table 8.6. Note that the data is discrete, because people can only enter a shop a definite number of times, e.g. 5 times or 6 times, not 5.1 or 5.2 or 5.3 times.

Table 8.6 Number of times the 200 customers visiting the dissertation department store entered the store in the previous 6 months

Number of visits made to the store	Number of customers
1	10
2	18
3	40
4	40
5	60
6	20
7	5
8	6
9	1
Total number of customers	**200**

Figure 8.6 An example of a column graph showing the number of visits made by 200 customers to the dissertation department store (based on data in Table 8.6)

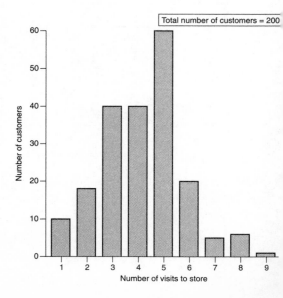

Figure 8.6 illustrates the data when drawn as a column graph. Because the data is discrete, each column is kept separate.

Isotypes (also termed pictographs)
This method of displaying data is extremely effective. In an isotype diagram the symbols used represent the subjects. For example, suppose a book shop wanted to display the number of books sold in a 5-year period, the results could look like Figure 8.7. Isotypes are interesting to look at and make a useful change. The main difficulty is finding a symbol that looks like the subject it represents. They need to be simple, easy to copy and instantly recognizable. Each symbol stands for a certain number. In Figure 8.7 each ⊞ represents 1,000 books, and half a symbol ▯ represents 500 books. Obviously isotypes cannot be used in every situation, and it is difficult to divide some symbols up accurately to represent small numbers such as 3, 4 or 5.

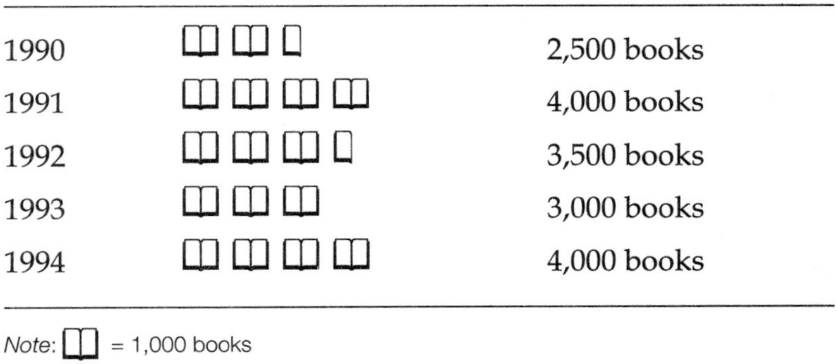

1990	⊞ ⊞ ▯	2,500 books
1991	⊞ ⊞ ⊞ ⊞	4,000 books
1992	⊞ ⊞ ⊞ ▯	3,500 books
1993	⊞ ⊞ ⊞	3,000 books
1994	⊞ ⊞ ⊞ ⊞	4,000 books

Note: ⊞ = 1,000 books

Figure 8.7 Number of books sold by a bookshop over the 5-year period from 1990 to 1994

Inferential statistics
Descriptive statistics are used to describe the data you collect. The pie chart (Figure 8.3) illustrates percentages in the different sectors of the sample. What the pie chart does not indicate is whether the percentages plotted in each sector are different because this represents the true situation and the shopping habits of customers, or whether they occurred just by chance alone on the day the survey was carried out. There is a special branch of statistics called inferential statistics which allows you to do this. Over the years statisticians have applied mathematical theory and have developed a range of procedures which, if followed, give a good indication

whether the quantitative results of any investigation have arisen by chance alone or represent true differences existing.

This chapter does not work through all the procedures in detail, since a number of excellent books are available (see Annotated bibliography). Instead, some of the main principles are explained, so if you need to use any statistical test you will know what to look for and have confidence you have selected the correct one. It is essential to decide, at the start of any data collection techniques, which statistical tests you intend to use. This is because certain tests only work with certain types of data, e.g. nominal, ordinal, interval, etc., and with a particular sample size. The population from which you collect the sample can also influence the type of test used.

Population and probability

Two important concepts associated with inferential statistics are those of population and probability. Mention has already been made of populations with respect to the selection of samples (see page 59). Statisticians use the word population in a different sense. With inferential statistics, if a particular test indicates that two (or more) sets of data, when analysed, are significantly different, it is concluded that the data has been taken from two different populations. If no significant difference exists, the data has been taken from the same population. Statisticians also apply the terms parametric and non-parametric with respect to populations. In a parametric population, the distribution of the characteristic being investigated, e.g. height, follows a particular distribution. Statisticians have identified a number of different types of population distribution: for example, normal, Poisson and binomial. A non-parametric population is where no assumption is made about the distribution of the characteristic in question. Again, the choice of statistical test which can be applied will depend on whether you are dealing with a parametric or non-parametric population.

Probability

The words 'significantly different' have been used a number of times in connection with inferential statistics. It is essential to realize that statistical tests do not prove or disprove anything. They give a measure of the probability of a particular situation arising by chance or some other cause.

The probability of the sun not rising tomorrow is 0, or in percentage terms 0%. Conversely, the probability that it will rise tomorrow is certain, or in percentage terms 100%. It is possible, therefore, to give a numerical value, usually as a percentage, to different levels of probability and statisticians have worked out theoretical probability tables for all the commonly used statistical tests. In general terms, business works to a probability (p) of 5%, or 0.05 as a decimal or 5:100 as a ratio. This is referred to as the 5% significance level. It means that in 95 cases out of 100 the differences observed are due to the real differences existing, but in 5 cases out of 100 they will have arisen by chance alone.

Tests of significance can also be used in respect of correlation, as opposed to difference, and probabilities have been calculated to show whether the relationship between two variables has occurred by chance, or whether there is a real relationship, and as one variable changes so does the other.

Procedure for carrying out statistical tests of significance

All tests are carried out using the same basic scheme as follows.

STAGE 1

Two hypotheses are set up. Statisticians refer to these as the *null hypothesis* (referred to as H_0) and the *alternative hypothesis* (referred to as H_1). The null hypothesis states that for the test being carried out, nothing special has occurred and no changes have taken place, i.e. no significant difference is present. The alternative hypothesis is that something special has occurred and a change has taken place, i.e. there is a significant difference.

STAGE 2

The chosen significance test is carried out and the appropriate statistic is calculated. This value is then compared to the critical value in the selected probability table appropriate to the chosen test.

STAGE 3

The calculated value and the theoretical critical value are compared. If the calculated value is less than the table's critical value, the null hypothesis (H_0) is not rejected. It is accepted and any differences are not significant; they could have happened by chance alone. However, if the calculated value is equal to, or greater than, that listed in the table, the null hypothesis (H_0) is rejected, and the alternative hypothesis is accepted. In other words, significant differences exist, they are not due to chance alone. In most tests a probability of 5% or 0.05 is used, which means that in 95 cases out of 100, real differences exist.

Examples of statistical tests

All are given in outline only. The Annotated bibliography lists books which give more detail.

NON-PARAMETRIC TESTS

These are tests which make no assumptions about the distribution of data. The tests work on either nominal or ordinal data.

- *Sign test*. This uses nominal data, and pairs of scores from repeated measures. It compares the number of differences between two conditions which are in the same direction. The null hypothesis states that there is no difference with respect to the scores. The alternative hypothesis states that there is a difference. An example would be a panel of people asked to compare an 'original' washing powder with a 'new improved' version of the same powder. The panel is asked to state if they feel the improved is better than the original, recording an improvement as (+) and no improvement as (−).

- *Wilcoxon signed rank test*. This uses data on the ordinal scale, and pairs of scores from repeated measures. The same null and alternative hypothesis are used as with the sign test. It is more sophisticated than the sign test, in that the differences are measured and then placed in rank order. With the above washing powder example, the volunteers would be asked to grade the improvement on a numerical scale, e.g. 1–5, and the values could then be ranked.

- *Mann Whitney U test*. An example would be a company with two separate factories, one having a greater absenteeism record than the other. Collected data needs to be ordinal. In the example the number of absences on a daily basis for a given time from each factory could be collected. The results from both factories could then be ranked as if one group, with the lowest number of absences recorded as one, and the highest number of absences being the top number. The null hypothesis would expect no differences, that is the scores would be randomly distributed across the two factories. If, however, most of the low-ranked scores came from one factory, and most of the high-ranked scores came from the other factory, this would signify that real differences exist between the two factories.

- *The Chi-squared test*. This is a popular test, and used a lot in market research. There are a number of variations, all of which use nominal data. It must be noted that chi-square does not work on individual scores, but frequencies, i.e., the number of times one event occurs. The basis of chi-square is that it compares the observed result with the expected result. In most calculations the expected result is 50–50. For example, suppose you carry out a survey to investigate people's preference for instant or real coffee, your observed results may be 70% of your sample prefer instant coffee and 30%, real coffee. You would regard your expected result as 50% like instant, and 50% like real coffee. You would then compare the observed results, i.e. 70% and 30% with the expected, i.e. 50% and 50%, and determine whether there was a significant difference.

PARAMETRIC TESTS

Tests in this group assume that the population has a particular distribution. Only interval and ratio data can be used. With some tests the sample size needs to be watched.

- *The Student's t test*. This test is well known, and is used to compare means from small samples, each usually less than 30. The test was first described in 1908 by W.S. Gosset. He worked for the Guinness family, and because he was not allowed to use his own name he published the work under the name of Student. The null hypothesis states that there are no significant differences between the means. There are variations of the t test, depending whether you are using paired or unpaired samples.

- *The Analysis of variance (ANOVA)*. This is a more complicated statistical procedure, and a number of variations exist. It is used when you want to compare two or more sample means to measure significant differences.

Concluding remarks

This chapter summarizes the main methods for interpreting the results of your research. Irrespective of whether you have used a qualitative or quantitative approach, remember that your judgement as an independent researcher is important. The results of your research, presented in the correct format, are the evidence to support your views and ideas.

9   Writing up your dissertation

Introduction

Finally, there comes a point when all the material has to be collated and written up to produce the final dissertation. A dissertation that is well written and presented creates a good impression. This is essential for getting your ideas and arguments across to the reader. On the other hand, poor writing and sloppy presentation distracts the reader, and this may count against you.

In most universities the production of a dissertation forms a major proportion of a student's final assessment. It examines a number of important skills including information retrieval, problem solving, academic criticism and communication. Many lecturers would argue that, irrespective of the subject, a dissertation is the best indicator of 'honours worthiness' in any degree programme. In reality, the dissertation can be a very unfair method of assessment, since it is only the final product, the written up and bound dissertation, that is marked. The processes you have gone through, the problems you may have faced and how you solved them, if not included in the final write up, may go unnoticed. Although in certain institutions the proposal and ongoing meetings with supervisors form part of the final mark, in many universities it is still only the final document that is assessed. The total process of writing up and producing the final dissertation is, therefore, very important. It must reflect the considerable effort and care you put into it.

As far as possible, the writing up should be completed as you go along. Writing is very much part of the total research process and many sections like the literature review may be in draft. You now need to pull all the sections together in order to produce the final copy. It is essential that the final version reads as one document; it should run smoothly from the first page to the last. What sometimes happens is that it may read as a number of separate sections only linked by a common author and title. Even though the dissertation is divided into separate chapters or sections, at the final writing up stage you must give it a coherence and sense of continuity.

What is the best approach to writing up your dissertation?

Plan a realistic time schedule for writing up, and then stick to it. Remember that this should include time for writing, typing up, printing out and binding your work. It is all too easy to fall behind schedule, and very difficult to catch up again.

Start writing up as soon as you have gathered any material, don't keep putting it off, or you will end up with huge amounts of data that are very difficult to sort out. If one aspect of the work is going slowly, don't be afraid to leave it for a few days, and return to it another time. Don't, however, use it as an excuse to stop work altogether, get on with writing up a different section. The change of material helps you see the overall context. Because dissertations are so long, you can often lose sight of this and can get bogged down in one section, especially if that section appears to be difficult to write.

Don't think of it as the final draft at this stage, just get your ideas down on paper. You can modify and improve it later. Don't spend hours perfecting one sentence – in the long run it is more effective to correct and change a first, but incomplete draft.

Always keep a note of any references you use, so that when you come to write your references and bibliography it will not be such a huge job. Academic referencing always seems to cause lots of problems, but in reality it can be straightforward, and full details on how to compile references are given at the end of this chapter.

If you do these things as you go along, by the time you are ready to refine the final draft, you will be able to concentrate on moulding your existing writing into an acceptable style, rather than having to start from scratch.

How to start writing up

Recounting the stages you have gone through and asking yourself some very basic questions will help clarify your thoughts at this stage.

- You have researched a particular topic that interested you. What attracted you to it in the first place and why was it your final choice? With hindsight, would you select it again?

- You have reviewed the literature. How did it inform your thinking and research design? Scan the research proposal. Have you achieved all your stated aims and objectives?
- What methodological approach did you take and why? Which particular data collection techniques and methods did you finally select? How have you analysed and interpreted the data? Do your findings support or refute a particular argument or theory?
- Do you think your work has been balanced? Did you remain objective throughout? Does it fit in and compare with the research of others?
- What general and specific conclusions has your research indicated? How do these relate back to the original research topic? Do they shed light or otherwise on any wider issues which may be involved?
- Would you say your research may influence a particular practice in a particular field of business and management?
- If you could go back right to the beginning equipped with the knowledge and experience you have gained, would you do it in exactly the same way or make changes?

Obviously, you are not going to be able to answer all of these questions, but going back to the start and thinking things through a second time can put them in perspective, and help you to see your dissertation as a whole.

Keep to the regulations

All universities have regulations with respect to the submission of dissertations. Don't assume that you will be allowed to deviate from these, you won't. The author knew a student who was not initially granted his degree, because his dissertation was bound in the wrong colour! He presented his work in black and the university regulations stipulated blue. He had to have his work rebound before he could graduate. Check on the following:

- *Submission date.* Does your dissertation have to be handed in by a certain date? Obtain a receipt when you hand it in.

- *Length.* What is the minimum and maximum word length? Does this include appendices, bibliography etc?

- *Declaration.* Most universities require the student to produce a signed and dated declaration that the work is all their own, and has not been previously submitted for another degree. All reference to other people's work must be acknowledged. Universities regard plagiarism as a very serious offence and, if proven, it will certainly stop you getting your degree.

- *Page layout.* Do you have to conform to any special page layout with respect to margin size, font size, single or double spacing, position of headers and footers, page numbering etc? All of these seem very minor points, but together are important to the overall presentation of your work.

- *Number of copies.* How many copies of the final work do you have to hand in?

- *Overall layout and structure.* Are you expected to follow a prescribed layout and arrange the various chapters in a particular order?

- *Binding.* Some universities expect undergraduate dissertations to be professionally bound like a book. Some allow spiral binding, and some let students hand in their work in a loose-leaf A4 ring folder.

- *Referencing system.* All references must be cited in the text, together with a bibliography. Are you expected to use a particular referencing system?

Characteristic features of academic writing – developing an appropriate good writing style

Academic writing is defined as follows:

- *somewhat specialized.* It is written for a specific audience and attempts to put forward a well-balanced view about the topic under investigation. It constantly refers to published work (with appropriate referencing), theory and results.

- *produced in an 'academic style'.* That is, the passive voice and third person are used (e.g. 'a survey was carried out' *not* 'I carried out a survey') when describing research and conclusions, and always uses evidence to back up theories and ideas. Practise writing up your work in the same manner. Once you start to think about writing in an academic style, and begin to use it, you will find it is easier to get your ideas across. It's worth mentioning here that certain areas (e.g. action research) now encourage writing in the first person – check with your supervisor what's best for you.

- *well planned and thought through.* Time spent at the early planning stages is never wasted. It will make your written argument more coherent and focused. Careful planning helps in formulating a logical sequence and stops you missing out certain pieces of important information.

- *coherent and has a strong direction.* Have all your data well organized, and you will be able to concentrate on the structuring of your arguments at the writing up stage. As you write, think about the argument you are trying to put across, and the questions you need to answer. This will keep your writing focused. Each topic should connect to the last one, so that a coherent argument is developed. Don't think of each section as an essay in itself; each theme should flow from the preceding one, and in this way you will find that the dissertation becomes a whole rather than a collection of disconnected themes. Always try to present a balanced discussion linking one section of your writing with the next. Use the format of the dissertation to help here. Give each part a short introduction to explain 'the story so far and where it's going'.

- *original, with no plagiarism or excessive paraphrase.* Always use your own words and never be tempted to copy out other people's writing. This is plagiarism. Plagiarism can be defined as taking and using someone else's writing, ideas or thoughts and passing them off as your own. When writing a dissertation you may come up against a difficult concept which you need to include, and at first glance it may seem a lot easier to copy out someone else's writing, or summarize, i.e. paraphrase their writing. The problem is that you will never understand the concept you are writing about. More importantly, if this is discovered when your dissertation is marked, the chances are you will fail your dissertation. Plagiarism and paraphrase are regarded as serious offences. Most universities come down heavily on the guilty student. What many students fail to realize is that although plagiarism is easy to do, it is extremely easy to recognize in a piece of writing. Plagiarized writing resembles a patchwork quilt; the styles change. Moreover, most of your lecturers have read for themselves the standard works in your subject, and the chances are they will be able to identify the original authors of the parts you have plagiarized.

    You must realize that it is perfectly permissible to use people's ideas and quotations, provided that you cite them in your writing. Academic writing always contains references to other published works. It gives your work credibility, as it shows you are aware of the current literature in your field of study. Published work can also be used as evidence to support your line of argument. There are different ways of citing other people's writing. The most popular is known as the Harvard system and this is explained later in this chapter.

• *well-presented, with correct spelling, grammar and punctuation.* Modern software packages and word processing facilities can help you make your dissertation look attractive and easy to read. A well-written document is better for being well produced and presented, and it is now possible to produce and print documents that were once in the realm of the professional printer. Good presentation, however, is not a substitute for good clear writing. Good writing involves using the correct grammar, spelling and punctuation. It is essential to get these correct if you want your writing to have academic credibility. Finally, don't go overboard with printer effects.. You are not producing a brochure to recommend a particular software package. Decide at the beginning the font size, the print style, layout of headings, etc. and be consistent all the way through your document. Don't rely entirely on spelling and grammar checkers now available on many word processing packages. Although they can check the spelling of words like practise and practice, stationery and stationary, discreet and discrete, there and their, the words are checked in isolation and not in context. For example, which of the following sentences is correct – 'The manager in charge of stationary had a discrete conversation about bad practise in his factory' or 'The manager in charge of stationery had a discreet conversation about bad practice in his factory'?

Dissertation format

Most business undergraduate programmes provide guidelines on how to set out a dissertation. If these are not available to you, the following scheme is suggested. Even with guidelines, the advice should prove useful.

The overall objective is to produce a clear, easy-to-follow document. A dissertation is presented in a series of headed chapters or sections. It should be an original piece of work which argues convincing and persuasive conclusions that have developed from a substantial body of collected data and material. The overall arrangement of a dissertation is best in three sections:

1. *Introductory chapters*

   These set out the relevant contextual and theoretical background information, and the reasons for studying the topic. They give an overview of the methodological approach and the data collection techniques used.

2. *Central and middle chapters*

   This is the main body of your dissertation. The exact number of sections or chapters will depend on the nature of your topic, but you would normally include the literature review, methodology and results. If you are adopting a case study approach involving a particular company or organization, you will need a section describing and explaining the example involved. With action research these middle sections could be in the form of a story or narrative.

3. *The concluding chapters*

   The final chapters, usually termed conclusion and discussion, pull the whole work together. They relate your research findings to the initial aims and objectives set out at the start. These concluding sections must present an overview of the preceding chapters without simply repeating earlier material. They should be used to reflect on the whole process of the dissertation, and attempt to explain where the research could lead if it was to be continued.

In addition to the above, the dissertation should contain a contents page, acknowledgements and a bibliography. A suggested, more detailed format is now given, in the order in which these features should appear, followed by specific advice for each section. Certain sections are sometimes known by alternative names and these are given in brackets.

Suggested format

Title page
Acknowledgements
Abstract
Contents page
Introduction (background to study)
Literature review
Methodology and data collection
Results (observations, findings)
Discussion

Conclusions (sometimes includes recommendations)
Bibliography (references cited)
Appendices

Depending on your dissertation, you may need a glossary of terms and abbreviations and a signed declaration that the work is your own. Some institutions require students to provide separate lists of tables and figures in addition to the contents page.

Title page
Here you include the title of the dissertation, your full name and, depending on your university, you may need to include details of your degree, enrolment number, and university department.

Acknowledgements
It is always a good idea to thank everyone who has helped you with your work. No-one likes being taken for granted. It is common practice to thank your supervisor and other members of the academic staff who may have provided extra support with particular sections. If you have worked in a company during the dissertation, e.g. on placement, don't forget to thank them as well. Always check the spellings of names, initials and qualifications of the people you include.

Abstract
The abstract should be a summary of the whole work. It should be brief, no more than a few hundred words, and to the point. It should contain no examples or other substantiating information, but simply be an outline of the work. An abstract should be complete in its own right. It is often easier to write the abstract when all the work is finished.

Contents page
All dissertations need a well laid out contents page. Usually chapters and sections are numbered using Arabic numbers (e.g. 1, 2, 3, etc.) and appendices in Roman numerals (e.g. I, II, etc.). The contents page is one of the first things the reader sees, but one of the last things that is written. It is important that it is accurate, so always double-check to ensure, for example, that Chapter 6 does really begin on page 45 and not 54. Errors like this creep in very easily towards the end of a piece of writing when you are tired and want to get it finished, but they do mar the overall impression of the work. With respect to numbering, page 1 normally starts at the introduction. The title page, acknowledgements, abstract, contents page are normally numbered i, ii, iii, etc.

Introduction

This should state clearly and concisely what it is you are setting out to achieve. The aim and plan of the dissertation should be made explicit here; do not spring any surprises on your reader later on. Tell the reader why you chose your topic, what the main research issues are, what aspects you investigated and how you investigated them.

Literature review

With every dissertation a review of previously published work is included. The review shows how your work relates to what other researchers have done. It sets your dissertation in the context of existing knowledge. Re-read the last two sentences and note the word 'relates' and the phrase 'context of existing knowledge'. With the literature review it is essential that you show quite clearly how your investigation compares and links with what has been done before. A review is not a catalogue of references arranged in chronological order, each one briefly summarized. Rather, your writing should pick out trends and patterns, giving and explaining reasons for and against a particular situation. It must relate theory to practice and argue why in certain situations established theories and ideas may or may not be accepted. In summary, it should provide a critical insight into the topic under investigation.

Methodology and data collection

In this section you describe and explain how you studied the topic of your investigation. Include a full account of your choice of techniques and whether you adopted a qualitative or quantitative approach. Each single method of data collection needs to be described, together with full information on any sampling technique you employed. Details of any pilots used should be included and how they may have influenced your final data collection. If triangulation was used, this also needs to be written up. Don't forget to include in this section the techniques used to interpret the collected data. The methodology section should be detailed enough for another researcher to repeat your work. The results they collect and their interpretation may be different, but this is another story. This section is often very straightforward and is a good place to begin writing the dissertation.

Results

Results can range from transcriptions of interviews to tables of raw data. This section only describes the results obtained. Refrain from explaining what they mean. This comes in the next section. It is very easy to comment on the results when describing them, but this can be confusing for the reader. In this section you would include a full analysis of how you interpreted the data and give details of any calculations. If you have collected data in a number of different ways, keep each one separate. In this section you can include tables and figures to summarize your quantitative results, and describe the trends and concepts identified from qualitative analysis. With certain quantitative investigations you may have collected vast amounts of data. In these situations summarize the data with the use of tables and only include the summaries in the main dissertation. The original data can either be included in an appendix or can be submitted as a separate file. It might be a good idea to discuss this with your dissertation supervisor.

Discussion

In this section you answer a number of questions. You interpret what your research findings mean and whether they agree with the aims and objectives set out in your proposal. You relate your work back to the literature review and see how it fits in with all the published work. How does it compare with established theories and ideas? Are there similarities and differences and why? If you have taken a grounded theory approach, how has the theory developed? Are there any generalizations you can make? You also need to include in the discussion an account of the appropriateness of your methodology and data collection techniques, and whether in hindsight they were the most suitable. The discussion is a very important section of the dissertation, and should also demonstrate how your research relates to the wider context of the subject. It is not an easy section to write, and is often best started by using a series of topic headings as a guide. These include:

- the relationship of the results to the objectives set out in the proposal;
- the relationship to published literature;
- the role of theory, grounded or otherwise;
- the appropriateness of the methodology and data collection;
- the effect on professional practice.

It is very easy when writing the discussion to include general points which, although important, do not arise from your work. You must base your writing in this section on the work you have done. Although you can use evidence from the literature, it must support your views and opinions. The conclusions must not become a summary of your work and other people's work. The two must integrate.

Conclusions

This is the final section, and because it is the last one it is important to write it as well as you can. Include the following elements:

- a summary of the principal features of your study;
- an outline of the main findings, key concepts and theories identified in the literature;
- the implications involved by reflecting on your study as a practitioner and a researcher;
- any recommendations for future research and practical suggestions which may influence the practice of business and management.

Bibliography

The bibliography should be presented according to a recognized academic format. The Harvard system described later is popular and recommended. Certain universities ask students to distinguish between references actually cited in the text and general works not cited which may have informed their thinking.

Appendices

If you have any material that you produced or gathered during the dissertation process which you feel is relevant, but would break up the flow of your argument if placed in the main text, then consider including it as an appendix. Any letters/replies, large amounts of data, copies of questionnaires and interview schedules, etc. that are too detailed to place in the main body of the work can be included as appendices. Do, however, be sparing in your use of appendices, don't include material simply to pad the work out. Only include essential information. Usually appendices are not included in the word length of a dissertation.

Other points

The following are general points which may also help at the writing up stage:

- *Format.* The unfamiliar format of a dissertation often causes problems. Having to write an abstract, contents page, acknowledgements, etc. can present some students with difficulties simply because they have not had to do them before. Most of these things should be left until the main body of the work has been written, so don't worry about them at first. Get started on your research, and as you read about your topic, and look at old dissertations in the library, you will gradually become more familiar with the format of a dissertation.

- *Word length.* Be aware of the required length of the dissertation, and estimate how many words you are going to include in each section. This way you can check as you go along whether your work is going to meet the required length at the end. Students who are used to writing shorter essays and reports are unfamiliar with producing a piece of work some 10,000–20,000 words long. In consequence they often produce a number of standard-length essays of about 2,000 words and try to fit them together to the required word length. This doesn't work, as the final dissertation does not hang together as one coherent piece of well-argued writing. You must ensure that each chapter follows on logically from the last, and that the whole work follows a line of argument from introduction to conclusion. A number of students become worried when they have too many words. This is a good position to be in; far better than to have too few words. It means you have a lot of information. A number of devices can sometimes help cut down the word number. For example, remove words like also, very, usually, often. This can save in total around 200 words. Flowcharts and diagrams can take the place of long descriptions. Finally, use appendices effectively.

- *Using tables and figures.* If your work would be made clearer and easier to understand through the use of a table or diagram (always called figures), etc. then include them. If you are putting one in to fill out a chapter, then don't include it. Make sure tables and figures are easy to understand, and help to explain your work. If they are irrelevant or superfluous they may confuse the reader and detract from your work. Also, they need to be referenced if taken from another source.

- *Being too descriptive.* The most common complaint about dissertations is that the writing is too descriptive. To avoid this error make sure you set out to prove something, and present evidence to back up your assertions. You should not simply describe something, but rather analyse it by saying why it is the way it is, and how it could be improved.

- *Using evidence.* Always use evidence to back up any assertions you make, and make it clear how you arrived at your conclusions. State clearly whether the evidence you use is your own, or if you are basing your conclusions on the work of others. If the latter is the case, make sure you include references to your sources. As mentioned before, avoid plagiarism at all times – if in doubt put in the appropriate reference; it is better to include too many than too few.

Advice on references, footnotes, quotations and other points of style

Quoting references

There are different ways of doing this and one of the most popular and universal methods in current use is the *Harvard system*. Here the author's surname and date of publication are used to identify a reference. In the text a reference would be cited as, 'some interesting results were obtained (White, 1985)'. If the author's surname is part of the sentence, then the date alone is sufficient, for example, 'White (1985) reported some interesting results'. It is customary to use parentheses as shown. If reference to a specific page or diagram is required, as opposed to the whole work, then the following technique applies, 'analysis of the results (White, 1985, p. 13, table 2)', or 'White (1985, p. 13, table 2) in his results indicated ...'.

At the end of the text the information sources are listed alphabetically by surnames. If the same author has published several works in one year they are identified as 1952a, 1952b, 1952c, and so on, both in the written text and in the reference list at the end of the writing. An advantage with this method is that references can be either easily added or removed.

Constructing the bibliography

The preparation of the bibliography always seems to present students with unnecessary difficulty. They are often uncertain as to how much detail for each reference should be included. Examples of different types of information sources are now given showing what details should be recorded, and how each could be set out in a list using the Harvard system. It is an accepted convention that certain words are underlined (if typed or hand written) or italicized (if word processed or printed). Some authors and publishers recommend slightly different ways of setting out from that given below: for example, the use of capital letters for author's names, enclosing dates of publication in parentheses, reversing the order of publisher and place of publication, and minor changes in punctuation. The important point is to adopt a system which provides enough detail so that the reader of your work could locate a copy of the same reference without undue difficulty.

EXAMPLES OF DETAILS TO RECORD

Textbook
Record: Author surname(s) and initial(s), date of publication, title of book, edition (except the first), place of publication and publisher. Include page numbers, tables and figures if mention has been made to specific parts of the book.

> Stannack, P. (1993) *Managing People for the First Time: Gaining Commitment and Improving Performance.* London: Pitman.

A paper in a periodical
Record: Author surname(s) and initial(s), date of publication, title of article, name of journal, volume (and part number if applicable), inclusive pages of paper.

> Harrigan, K.R. (1985) An Application of Clustering for Strategic Group Analysis. *Strategic Management Journal*, Vol. 6, pp. 55–73.

Some journals have long titles and some form of abbreviation is acceptable. However, never make up your own, since if everyone did this, it would soon cause chaos and confusion. To be on the safe side never use abbreviations and give journal titles in full.

A book with every chapter written by a different author
Many books have each chapter written by a different author, and the whole book is edited by someone else. In these instances record, for the chapters used, author surname(s) and initial(s), date of publication, title of chapter, page number(s), editor'(s') surname(s) and initial(s), title of book, place of publication, publisher.

> Eisenhardt, K.M. (1995) Building Theories from Case Study Research, pp. 65–90 in Huber, G.P. and Van de Ven, A.H. (eds) *Longitudinal Field Research Methods: Studying Processes of Organizational Change.* London: Sage.

A thesis
Record: Author surname(s) and initial(s), date, title of thesis, degree awarded, academic institution awarding the degree.

> Ritson, M.B. (1996) The Interpretation of Advertising Meaning. PhD thesis. University of Lancaster.

A report
Various types of reports are available, but they can be extremely difficult to trace, since many writers give too little information in their reference lists. Always provide enough detail. If the report has been the responsibility of a particular person (normally the chair-person of the committee writing the report) then classify the report according to their surname.

> Taylor, F.J.W. (1994) *Management Development to the Millennium. The Taylor Working Party Report. The Way Ahead 1994–2001.* Corby: The Institute of Management.

If the report has been prepared for an official organization, and the authorship is uncertain, then use the name of the organization in quoting and listing the reference. For example,

> Advisory Board for the Research Councils (1983) *Scientific Opportunities and the Research Budget: A Report to the Secretary for Education and Science.* London: Department of Education and Science.

Unsigned articles in books, journals, newspapers etc.
Often articles appear and the author's name cannot be traced. Refer to such articles, both in the text and the reference list, as anonymous together with their date. The word 'anonymous' may be abbreviated to 'anon'.

> Anon (1994) The Iron is Cold. *The Economist.* Vol. 30, No. 7848 (29 January), p.46.

Other books (e.g. data books, directories)
With certain types of reference book it is difficult to find the name of either the editor or author. In such cases give as much detail as possible.

Unpublished information
Although the majority of references will be from published material, occasionally you may learn of some interesting work possibly in a letter

from, or during a conversation with, someone. It is acceptable to use this information, provided the person in question has no objection, and you keep this type of reference source to a minimum. Written work relying completely on information from unpublished work would lack credibility. Refer to this type of information source as a personal communication. In the text it would be acknowledged as, 'the results of the survey were not significant' (personal communication, 1987)'.

In the reference list the reference should be filed alphabetically under 'P', together with a short description as to the type of communication, for example, 'a letter' or 'conversation'. Many professional publishers instruct their authors to cite this type of source only in the text, and not include it in the reference list. For student work, however, it is good practice to include it as it shows to either a reader or examiner that you have consulted a wide variety of different sources.

Non-book sources
With this type of information source give as many details as possible. For example, with audiovisual material record the title, distribution or production company, date of production or release, production personnel, namely director and producer, and type of material (e.g. film, video, tape, slides). In practice, all this information may not be available, so record as much as you can.

Citing electronic sources
No official method has been adopted yet, and the following examples are guidelines only:

E-mail correspondence: Sender, sender's e-mail address, subject, date.
Electronic journal: Author, date, title of article, journal title, volume, location, URL.
Internet site: Author/editor, date, title, location of server, publisher/maintainer of site, URL.

As with citing traditional sources, it is important to be as consistent as possible. The technology is advancing all the time. When quoting electronic sources, try to include as much information as possible so the reader could locate the same source.

Footnotes
In academic writing footnotes are sometimes used to explain an unusual phrase or unfamiliar term, or to add extra information which would be awkward to include in the text. Footnotes are either

asterisked or numbered. The numbering is either consecutive throughout the text, or at the start of each page or chapter. Try to keep footnotes down to a minimum. Footnote numbers can cause confusion and if the work is being typed or word-processed, the spacing of the footnotes at the bottom of the page can be difficult. Social science and humanity students make great use of footnotes and sometimes use them to quote all their references.

Use of et al.

Articles and books are sometimes written by more than one author. If there are more than three authors (e.g. Machon, Walker, Holmes, and Nyland) the *et al.* (= *et alia*, Latin 'and others') can be used instead of quoting all four names. The reference would be referred to by the first author's name followed by *et al.*, for instance, Machon *et al.* The reference is quoted in this form in the text, but in full in the bibliography. The *et al.* is always underlined or printed in italics, and is always followed by a full stop.

Use of quotations

It is perfectly acceptable to use quotations to illustrate a particular point in your writing. Always keep each quotation to a minimum and normally no longer than two or three lines. Quotations of a paragraph or longer are best left out unless there is a particular reason to include them. Always quote correctly, and acknowledge either the source or reference. It improves the presentation if each quotation is indented slightly, and separated from the rest of the writing. Use single quotation marks at the beginning and end of each quotation. Students often fail to realize they can amend quotations to make them more relevant to the writing at hand. For instance, use square brackets if you wish to add something not present in the original quotation, but which would make its meaning clearer. For example,

'They [the unions] gave their approval to the decision'.

If the original author has made a mistake then use *sic* (Latin, meaning 'so written') to show there was an error in the original and you have not misquoted:

'The paper (*sic*) were put into the file'.

Here *sic* means that 'papers' should be read instead of 'paper'. Note *sic* is always underlined or italicized.

If you want to shorten a quotation, but wish to include some of it, then use ... (three dots). For example:

'The cat ... on the mat'.

Use of op. cit. *and* ibid.

Op. cit. and *ibid.* tend to be used mainly by humanities students either in footnotes or reference lists.

When used, both *op. cit.* and *ibid.* are always underlined or italicized. *Op. cit.* (= *opere citato*, Latin meaning 'in the work cited') is used when you are referring to a reference which has been mentioned earlier in the text, for instance, White, *op. cit.*, p. 132. *Ibid.* (= *ibidem*, Latin meaning 'in the same place') is used in a footnote or reference list if consecutive references have the same source even though the page numbers, etc. may be different.

And finally

Enjoy the writing process. Although it is hard work, it is rewarding, and a well-written, neatly presented document gives a great feeling of satisfaction.

10 The role of supervisors and the assessment of dissertations

Introduction

This chapter is about the help universities give to students preparing dissertations and how the final product is assessed.

The role of supervisors

Although the dissertation is an independent piece of work, universities realize that students need support in its preparation and writing up. In most institutions you will be allocated a supervisor: a member of the teaching staff who will help and advise you. Once you are allocated your supervisor it is your responsibility to contact them, as they don't normally chase up students. See your supervisor regularly and establish a good, professional working relationship. Many students don't do this and the lack of useful advice often results in a poor dissertation. Simple things like keeping appointments, doing any set tasks and getting work in on time all help. Remember that staff usually supervise a number of students on top of a teaching, administrative and research workload. Students, therefore, turning up unannounced expecting the red carpet treatment are not welcome. When you see your supervisor for the first time, agree between you whether it is better to have meetings weekly, fortnightly or monthly, etc. As your dissertation progresses you may need to see your supervisor more or less frequently, depending on your needs. Lecturers realize this, since most of them at some time have written their own dissertations, and, as a result, are usually more than willing to accommodate the hard-working, motivated student. Regard the meetings with your supervisor as a real chance to engage in some meaningful academic debate. It is really a type of learning contract.

In certain universities meetings between student and supervisor can be very formal and supervision codes of practice are published. Following each meeting notes are made or a form filled in to record the points discussed. In some universities the record is signed by supervisor and student, with a copy given to the student and one put into the student's file. At other universities a more informal process occurs. In this situation it's a good idea to write down at the end of each supervisory meeting a summary of the points discussed, and what specific things you need to do before the next session. Between visits draft an informal agenda of issues to discuss next time.

The following section highlights what supervisors will and will not do. Possibly another way of looking at this is what students expect of their supervisors and what supervisors expect of their students.

What supervisors will do

- Encourage you to do well.
- Help and support you when things go wrong.
- Identify gaps in your knowledge and help you to put them right.
- Identify extra skills that you need and advise on how to acquire them.
- Advise on planning, methodology and the interpretation of results.
- Check and monitor progress by reading and commenting on drafts of chapters and sections of the dissertation. Remember it takes time to read a dissertation; so give them plenty of time to understand and comment on your work.
- Remind you of dates when work has to be finished.
- Open doors by introducing you to other members of staff who may give specific help with certain parts or chapters requiring specialist treatment, like data analysis or statistics.
- Be constructively critical of the work and offer helpful suggestions. However, be prepared to challenge new ideas and defend your own!

What supervisors won't do

- The work! It is your dissertation, not theirs.
- Write the dissertation for you. Supervisors will read sections and comment on general points, for example, how the argument is constructed, but don't expect them to re-write every sentence, or correct misspellings and grammatical errors.

- Do all the worrying. Supervisors are naturally concerned when things start to go wrong, and will try and help the conscientious, hard-working student. However, if you lack motivation and have a couldn't-care-less attitude, don't be surprised if you get a somewhat cool reception the next time you visit your supervisor.
- Give orders. Supervisors will suggest how to approach a problem and may indicate the advantages and limitations of particular methods and approaches. They expect you to consider their advice seriously, but they respect that it is the student's final decision.

The assessment of dissertations

Students often ask how dissertations are marked and graded. A brief account of how this takes place and the standard expected may help in the final stages of producing a dissertation. Mention has already been made that in some ways the whole process of assessing a dissertation is unfair. In the majority of universities it is only the product, the completed piece of work you submit, that is marked. The amount of time you have spent preparing the dissertation is not reflected in the final mark. In some universities, however, the proposal stage is graded and a record is kept of your meetings with your supervisors.

Procedures of marking

In most cases a dissertation is marked by two members of staff. The first marker is normally your supervisor and the second marker is another lecturer who has an expertise in the overall subject area of your dissertation. Each marker usually marks independently, and then they meet to agree the final mark. In most UK institutions dissertations scoring over 70% are graded first class, 60–69% are graded upper second class, 50–59% are graded lower second class and 40–49% are graded third class. Dissertations scoring below 40% are either recorded as a fail or a pass, depending on different university regulations.

There is also the system of external examiners. A selection of undergraduate dissertations are sent to the external examiner who vets the overall standard of marking to ensure parity between students. In some universities students are also asked to give a presentation about their dissertation, and attend a *viva voce* where they are questioned about their work.

What examiners look for when they mark

Examiners use assessment criteria against which to judge a student's work. Obviously the detailed procedure in your university will vary according to the course regulations, but the following general criteria may help you gauge the standard of your dissertation:

- Is the dissertation thoroughly related to the area of business and management studies?
- Has a range of primary and secondary sources been used, and what is the relevance of this material?
- To what extent has the role of theory played a part in the dissertation?
- Does the dissertation relate to the premise set out in the introduction?
- Is there a critical review of the literature of the subject?
- Has there been a critical engagement with the topic?
- Have the methodology and data collection methods been appropriate, and has the rationale for their selection been well argued?
- Are the research findings clearly explained and easy to understand?
- Have the findings been subjected to an appropriate method of analysis?
- Is there validity in the conclusions and recommendations reached? Have they been logically derived and fully supported by the evidence presented?
- To what extent does the dissertation demonstrate aspects of originality and contribution to knowledge?
- Is there quality in the way the dissertation is presented? Is it fully documented in an appropriate academic style, and is the text free from errors of spelling, punctuation and grammar?

If you have to give a presentation, or attend a *viva,* there are other criteria which need to be satisfied. With respect to a presentation don't forget that marks will be awarded for your style of presenting, as well as the content. Presentation skills are very important in the world of business, and most contemporary business studies programmes offer sessions in presenting. For extra advice on presentations see White (1991). At a *viva* you will be asked a series of questions which will examine the criteria listed above. Students are often asked what changes they would make in their dissertation if they could begin again, and where they would like the research to go if they were given the opportunity to continue. Remember in a *viva* you know the dissertation better than anyone, and, therefore, have the advantage.

Concluding remarks

This book has been written to help students prepare their dissertations. All the main stages have been worked through, and useful advice has been given. It is hoped that the advice isn't seen as patronizing in the sense of condescension. Patronizing also means to encourage and support, and the book has been written with this in mind.

The best of luck with your dissertation!

11 Specialist subject advice

Introduction

This chapter provides some information on a variety of popular subjects associated with business and management. The aim is not to provide detailed accounts of marketing, strategic management and the like, but present a series of key points that could form the basis of a dissertation. Examples of potential dissertation titles are also given.

Marketing

KEY POINTS

- Marketing strategy
- Product life cycle
- Positioning in the market
- Distribution and logistics
- Advertising
- Promotions
- Pricing
- Marketing economics

POTENTIAL DISSERTATION TITLES

An investigation into the marketing of non-profit-making organizations

A comparative study of marketing theory and the actual marketing of a youth employment training scheme

Strategy and policy-making

KEY POINTS

- The nature of strategy and strategic planning and policy-making
- The formulation and implementation of policy
- Integration and expansion strategies
- Competitive strategies
- The effect on people
- Globalization
- Different models of strategy

POTENTIAL DISSERTATION TITLES

*An investigation into the strategy of
business process re-engineering*

*An analysis of the development of the corporate strategy of a
named multinational company*

Finance and accounting

KEY POINTS

- Financial strategies
- Control
- Incentives
- Financial planning – short- and long-term
- Budgetary control
- Investments
- Financial decision-making
- Mergers and acquisitions

POTENTIAL DISSERTATION TITLES

*An investigation into the factors involved when
two companies merge*

*A comparative study of the banking services provided
today with those of 20 years ago*

Human resource management

KEY POINTS

- Appraisal
- Leader or manager?
- Equal opportunities
- The importance of minorities
- Self-development
- Job design
- Skills and competencies
- The role of teams

POTENTIAL DISSERTATION TITLES

An investigation into the function of the human resources department of a named company with respect to the needs of middle management

Are leaders born or bred? An investigation into the characteristics of leadership

Resource management

KEY POINTS

- Information systems
- The design and implementation of a management information system
- What is information?
- Principles of management information systems
- How to put resource management into practice

POTENTIAL DISSERTATION TITLES

An introduction to electronic data exchange: a study of the factors involved with respect to a named company

An evaluation of an introduction of management information systems into a small, traditional, family-run business

Managing change

KEY POINTS

- Innovation
- The factors involved in managing change
- Change at a department and company level
- Strategies to implement change and cope with change
- The introduction of change
- Communicating change
- Staff development issues

POTENTIAL DISSERTATION TITLES

*Managing change in the National Health Service:
a case study approach*

*An evaluation of changes in UK higher education policy
with respect to the 'new' universities*

Total quality management

KEY POINTS

- What is TQM?
- Standards – national and international
- Factors influencing the introduction of TQM
- The effect on the client
- The effect on the staff
- The meaning of quality
- Audits on quality

POTENTIAL DISSERTATION TITLES

*An analysis of the implementation of TQM
within the leisure industry*

*Investors in People: a study into the factors influencing
its introduction into a public sector organization*

International business

KEY POINTS

- Globalization
- The implications of international activities
- The EU and its implications
- Managing people and the influence of different cultures and language
- Communication across frontiers
- International competition
- Financial considerations
- The importance of information technology

POTENTIAL DISSERTATION TITLES

A comparative study showing how the image of a multinational company changes from country to country

An investigation into selected world-wide brands and their impact on the global market

Ethics and business

KEY POINTS

- The social responsibility of companies
- The role of stakeholders
- Environmental issues, e.g. pollution, toxic waste dumping
- The role of the individual vs the role of the organization
- The philosophical framework of ethics in business
- Relativism – natural law, utilitarianism and universalism

POTENTIAL DISSERTATION TITLES

The ethics of fund raising – an investigation into the practices of a large named charity

An evaluation of the marketing of genetically modified foods – is this an ethical problem?

12   Annotated bibliography

The following texts have been selected in case you need extra help with certain parts of your dissertation. From experience, students have found them easy to follow and understand. Although the details were correct at the time of writing, it's always worth checking to see if later editions are available. Also, new books are coming out all the time so be aware of new stock arriving in the library. If there is anything in particular to highlight about a book a comment is made. All the references cited in previous chapters are listed here.

General research books

A number of general texts on various aspects of research are on the market. They all cover the basic topics like proposals, data collection, writing up and the use of literature.

Blaxter, L., Hughes, C. and Tight, M. (1996)
How to Research
Buckingham: Open University Press

This book has good sections on the ethical issues of research and action research.

Dane, F.C. (1990)
Research Methods
California: Brooks and Cole

Denscombe, M. (1998)
The Good Research Guide for Small-Scale Social Research Projects
Buckingham: Open University Press

Hoffmann, A. (1996)
Research for Writers (5th edition)
London: A & C Black

Although written for the professional writer, this book contains lots of useful advice about collecting information. It gives addresses of copyright and specialist libraries. Well worth a look.

Johnson, D. (1994)
Research Methods in Educational Management
London: Longman

Although written for the education market there are easy-to-follow chapters on most aspects of research, including action research and case studies.

Marshall, P. (1997)
Research Methods: How to Design and Conduct a Successful Project
Plymouth: How To Books

A small book, but it is well indexed and there is a useful glossary. There are good chapters on sampling and analysing data.

Parsons, C.J. (1976)
Theses and Project Work
London: Allen & Unwin

This contains a short section on what to do at a *viva*.

Preece, R. (1994)
*Starting Research: An Introduction to
    Academic Research and Dissertation
    Writing*
London: Pinter Publishers

This title contains sections on the 'scientific method' and the understanding of statistics.

Sharp, J.A. and Howard, K. (1996)
*The Management of a Student Research
    Project* (2nd edition)
Aldershot: Gower

This book contains good sections on the use of literature, data collection and analysis.

White, B. (1991)
*Studying for Science: A Guide to
    Information, Communication and
    Study Techniques*
London: E. & F. N. Spon

Although written for science students, there are lots of chapters on general study skills. Chapter 8 is about presentation skills, and may be useful if you have to give a presentation as part of your dissertation assessment.

Business and management research books

There are a number of titles that specialize in the areas of business and management research methods.

Churchill Jr, G.A. (1995)
*Marketing Research: Methodological
    Foundations* (6th edition)
Fort Worth: The Dryden Press

Easterby-Smith, M., Thorpe, R. and
    Lowe, A. (1991)
Management Research: An Introduction
London: Sage

Gill, J. and Johnson, P. (1991)
Research Methods for Managers
London: Paul Chapman

Saunders, M., Lewis, P. and Thornhill,
    A. (1997)
Research Methods for Business Students
London: Pitman

Zikmund, W.G. (1994)
Business Research Methods (4th
    edition)
Fort Worth: The Dryden Press

In addition, the following general business and management books are useful in giving overviews on management ideas, thinking and techniques. They can help in generating the original dissertation idea.

Armstrong, M. (1986)
A Handbook of Management Techniques
London: Kogan Page

Crainer, S. (1996)
*Key Management Ideas: Thinkers that
    Changed the Management World*
London: Financial Times, Pitman,
    Management Master Class

Crainer, S. (1997)
*The Ultimate Business Library: 50 Books
    that Made Management*
Oxford: Capstone

Kennedy, C. (1993)
*Guide to the Management Gurus –
    Shortcuts to the Ideas of Leading
    Management Thinkers*
London: Century Business Books

Qualitative and quantitative books

The following are useful if you need particular help with specific techniques:

Bannister, P., Burman, E., Parker, I.,
    Taylor, M. and Tindall, C. (1994)
*Qualitative Methods in Psychology: a
    Research Guide*
Buckingham: Open University Press

Don't let the title put you off. There are excellent chapters on observation, interviews, and action research. Each chapter is well referenced.

Creswell, J.W. (1994)
Research Design: Qualitative and
*   Quantitative Approaches*
London: Sage

Although written for the
postgraduate market there are useful
sections on overall design and
experiments.

The Complete Survey Kit
London: Sage

A 9-volume set, written by a number
of people, covering every aspect of
carrying out a survey.

Denzin, N.K. and Lincoln, Y.S. (eds)
    (1994)
Handbook of Qualitative Research
London: Sage

This contains a wealth of information
about the techniques available.

Glaser, B. and Strauss, A. (1967)
The Discovery of Grounded Theory
Chicago: Aldine

Mason, J. (1996)
Qualitative Researching
London: Sage

This is a good book covering all the
main qualitative techniques needed.
It is well indexed.

Morgan, D.L. and Kruger, R.A. (1998)
The Focus Group Kit
London: Sage

This is a 6-volume collection detailing
all you need to know about focus
groups.

Munn, P. and Drever, E. (1990)
Using Questionnaires in Small Scale
*   Research: A Teacher's Guide*
Edinburgh: The Scottish Council for
    Research in Education

Although written for school teachers,
this is an excellent guide covering all
aspects of questionnaire research.

Robson, C. (1993)
Real World Research
Oxford: Blackwell

Statistics books

The titles below are useful if you
need additional help with quantitative analysis. All of them give
worked examples of the various tests
of significance you may need.

Harper, W.M. (1991)
Statistics (6th edition)
London: Longman

This is an excellent book, and has
good sections on the drawing of
tables and figures.

Malim, T. and Birch, A. (1997)
Research Methods and Statistics
London: Macmillan

Although written for psychology
students, this is a very easy book to
read. There are some excellent
sections on how to carry out the
statistical tests.

Sirkin, R.M. (1995)
Statistics for the Social Sciences
London: Sage

This is a very detailed text, and is best
used as a reference book.

Waters, D. (1998)
Essential Quantitative Methods: A Guide
*   for Business*
New York: Addison-Wesley Longman

Wright, D.B. (1997)
Understanding Statistics: An
*   Introduction for the Social Sciences*
London: Sage

Writing up books

The following give advice about the
writing up stage.

Legat, M.L. (1989)
The Nuts and Bolts of Writing
London: Robert Hale

A useful little book with easy-to-
follow chapters on punctuation,
spelling and style.

Lester, J.D. (1996)
Writing Research Papers: A Complete Guide (8th edition)
London: HarperCollins

This contains lots of material and there is a useful guide on using and citing electronic information.

Swetnam, D. (1997)
Writing Your Dissertation (2nd edition)
Oxford: How To Books

Turk, C. and Kirkman, J. (1984)
Effective Writing: Improving Scientific, Technical and Business Communication (2nd edition)
London: E. & F. N. Spon

Other references cited

Avery, C. and Zabel, D. (1997)
The Quality Managment Sourcebook: An International Guide to Material and Resources
London: Routledge

Barrett, D. and Peel, V. (1996)
Business Journals at SRIS
London: British Library

Brealey, R. and Edward, H. (1991)
A Bibliography of Finance
London: Massachusetts Institute of Technology Press

British Books in Print
London: J. Whitaker

British Catalogue of Audio Visual Material
London: British Library

British National Bibliography
London: British Library

British National Film and Video Catalogue
London: British Film Institute

British Reports: Translations and Theses
Boston Spa: BLDSC

Butcher, D. (1991)
Official Publications in Britain (2nd edition)
London: Library Association Publishing

Catalogue of Official Publications not Published by HMSO
Cambridge: Chadwick-Healey

Clough, R. (1995)
Japanese Business Information: An Introduction
London: British Library

Current Research in Britain
Boston Spa: BLDSC

Current Serials Received
Boston Spa: BLDSC

Dale, P. (ed.) (1993)
Guide to Libraries in Key UK Companies
London: British Library

Dale, P. (ed.) (1998)
Guide to Libraries and Information Units in Government Departments and Other Organisations
London: British Library

Elliott, J. (1980)
Action Research in Schools: Some Guidelines
Classroom Action Research Network Bulletin, No. 4
Norwich: University of East Anglia

Goodall, F., Gourvish, T. and Tolliday, S. (1997)
International Bibliography of Business History
London: Routledge

Halsey, A.H. (ed.) (1972)
Educational Priority: Volume 1: E.P.A. Problems amd Policies
London: HMSO

Henderson, C.A.P. (1998)
Councils, Committees and Boards, Including Government Agencies and Authorities: A Handbook of Advisory, Consultative, Executive, Regulatory and Similar Bodies in British Public Life
Beckenham: CBD Research Ltd

Henderson, S.P.A. and Henderson, A.J.W. (eds) (1998)
Directory of British Associations and Associations in Ireland (14th edition)
Beckenham: CBD Research Ltd

HMSO Annual Catalogue
London: HMSO

Index to Conferences Proceedings Received
Boston Spa: BLDSC

Index to Theses
London: ASLIB

Index Translationum: International
Paris: UNESCO

The International Directory of Business Information Sources and Services (2nd edition) (1996)
London: Europa

Journals in Translation
Boston Spa: BLDSC

Key British Enterprises
London: Dun & Bradstreet

Kompass Register
East Grinstead: Kompass Publishers Ltd

Lane, T. and Roberts, K. (1971)
Strike at Pilkingtons
London: Fontana

Leyden, M. and Lee, L. (eds) (1994)
Market Research: A Guide to the British Library Collections
London: British Library

Lowe, R. and Gilligan, C. (1995)
Revitalising the SME Sector through Focused Building Support Strategies.
British Academy of Management Annual Conference 1995.
Conference Proceedings, Sheffield, pp. 13–21

Mayo, E. (1933)
The Human Problems of an Industrial Civilisation
London: Macmillan

Mintzberg, H. (1973)
The Nature of Managerial Work
New York: Harper and Row

Museums Year Book Including a Directory of Museums and Galleries of the British Isles
London: The Museum Association

Newton, D.C. (1991)
Trademarks: An Introductory Guide and Bibliography (2nd edition)
London: British Library

Rapoport, R.N. (1970)
Three Dilemmas in Action Research.
Human Relations, Vol. 23, No. 6, pp. 499–513

Reynard, K.W. and Reynard, J.M.E. (eds) (1998)
ASLIB Directory of Information Sources in the United Kingdom (10th edition)
London: ASLIB

Rhodes, J. and Fallone, E. (1998)
Information on Standards: A Guide to Sources
London: British Library and the National Library of Scotland

Rimmer, B.M. (1992)
International Guide to Official Industrial Property Publications (3rd edition)
London: British Library

Spencer, N. (ed.) (1995)
How to Find Information – Business: A Guide to Searching in Published Sources
London: British Library

Spencer, N. (ed.) (1998)
The Instant Guide to Company Information On-Line: Europe
London: British Library

van Dulken, D. (1998)
Introduction to Patents Information (3rd edition)
London: British Library

Who Owns Whom?
London: Dun & Bradstreet

Who's Who
London: A. & C. Black

Index